California Maritime Academy Library (CSU)
3 0060 00040086 9

D0031388

WITHDRAWN

Origins of Sea Terms

THE AMERICAN MARITIME LIBRARY: VOLUME XI

Origins of Sea Terms

by *John G. Rogers*

Mystic Seaport Museum, Incorporated

Text set in Garamond Condensed
by Mim-G Studios, Inc.
Westerly, Rhode Island

Printed by Nimrod Press
Boston, Massachusetts

Bound by New Hampshire Bindery, Inc.
Concord, New Hampshire

Designed by Marie-Louise Scull

ISBN 0-913372-31-5

Dedication

This book
and the work that went into it
are dedicated to
my dear, patient and enthusiastic
wife and offspring,
and to all my other shipmates
through the years.

Contents

Preface

This book is intended for the enjoyment, and perhaps the enlightenment, of anyone interested in the rich lore of ships, boats, and the sea. It is my hope that it will be valued by professionals and amateurs alike, whether they be active, or "rocking-chair" sailors. It is a glossary, but, as you will see, the definitions are purposely very short as the emphasis is on origins. You will find, perhaps to your surprise, that some terms can even be traced to the Egyptians and the Phoenicians. And many words demonstrate how seamen many years ago covered surprising distances, with two-way influence with other cultures.

It all began for me with an idle thought stemming from a long-time fascination with sailors' language. "Where," said I, on seeing a couple of sailors walking down the street some years ago, "do you suppose the word 'peajacket' came from?" From there it wasn't long before I was "full and by."

Another factor in my interest was a remark in a book by the etymologist Mario Pei, that someday soon there may be a truly international language, perhaps even by the end of the XX century. I believe there is such a language now, in its own small substructure of world society — that of the mariner. Unlike other aspects of English-English, vis-a-vis American-English, where there are many differences, in sailors' English there are almost no such differences, except for local terms. Furthermore, if you step on board a large merchant ship of almost any flag, you will probably see the safety, operational, and principal compartment nameplates in two languages, English and its own native language. (If there is only one language, it's usually English!) And, in the Red Sea, you might hear a Greek officer conversing with a Jordanian pilot, or in Le Havre a Danish captain talking with a French tugboat skipper in — you guessed it — English. About mariners' American-English: it came to us from Britain, along with its parent language, for obvious reasons that need no enlargement here. Where it came from farther back is another story. Until about the X century, the inhabitants of the British

Isles were not seafarers to any extent — unlike their neighbors in Scandinavia, who had been since the V century. They became so in defense against the Viking raiders, and partly too because a relatively large number of Danes and Norwegians settled there and continued in their maritime activities. The inference of the strong influence of the old Nordic tongues seems clear. That of the French was also very important; it all began with the Norman invasion (1066) and continued as a result of the various Anglo-French wars and insurgences of the next three hundred years. French was for a time in some places in England both the official and the intellectual's language.

Another scholar, Logan Pearsall Smith, wrote that each type of human activity has its own vocabulary, for its materials, methods, instruction and problems; and that many of these terms find their way into the general language. One chapter in his book *Words and Idioms* is on sea terms, and another lists over a hundred of these that have indeed "come ashore."

Mariners' language, as well as our own general language, has always reflected changing conditions, and will continue to do so. It is interesting to see how many words that originated in the days of the simplest rigs have survived to this day — and just think of the degree of technical sophistication in large vessels and small, just since World War II!

The terms and phrases I have chosen fall into two groups, the largest of which comprises those in current use, the smaller, those you might see in reading about craft of yesteryear, or in model-making, or prowling in a museum. The list is pretty general, and usually pertains to on-board life. But I do include a few pertaining to the navy, weather, shipbuilding, astronomy, engineering, etc., when these relate to a sailor's regular activities.

I paraphrase two renowned scholars of our language: Dr. Eric Partridge quoting Dr. Ben Johnson, "dictionaries are like watches: the worst is better than none, and even the best cannot be expected to be quite true"; and Wilfred

Funk, who said that to do a complete listing would be almost impossible, that selections must be arbitrary and are sometimes accidental. There will be omissions, some by design and some by inadvertance.

To this I would like to add that I have used the best sources I could find, and I believe my "authorities" are sound. However, the reader should keep in mind three things about seamen. First, until fairly recently only a small percentage were even literate, let alone truly educated. Secondly, crews were, and still are, made up of men of several nationalities, regardless of ships' "flags." For these reasons, seamen's terminology was passed along largely by word-of-mouth, and no doubt with some variations. Furthermore, sailors, like others working in adverse conditions, developed a sense of humor about their lot, assigning many nicknames, some whimsical, that have persisted in their language, such as "honey barge" and "rose box" for example. (These were undoubtedly flavored by some adjectives you will not find in this book.)

Most scholars consider etymology a science. This work contains some etymology; but I should emphasize that, as in piloting in fog or uncertain currents, it also contains a lot of educated guessing.

Acknowledgments

I wish to express my hearty thanks for much invaluable encouragement, interest and help, without which this work would have been more difficult and less thorough; especially from:

Comdr. R. T. E. Bowler U.S.N.(Ret.)
Mr. Peter Davison
Vice Adm. William H. Groverman U.S.N.(Ret.)
Mr. J. Welles Henderson, Jr.
Mr. William P. Hunnewell
Mr. Karl Kortum
Mr. Philip E. Lilienthal
Mr. James A. McCurdy
Mr. William McKay
Capt. William N. Mills
Capt. John V. Noel U.S.N.(Ret.)
Capt. Donald V. Reardon U.S.C.G.(Ret.)
Mr. Henry Rusk
Mr. Harlan Soeten
Mr. P. C. F. Smith
Dr. Vernon Tate
Mr. Warwick W. Tompkins, Jr.
Capt. Neville E. Upham
Capt. Alan J. Villiers
Mr. William T. Wallace
Mrs. Natasha Wilkinson
Hart Museum, Mass. Institute of Technology, *Cambridge, Mass.*
Mariners' Museum, *Newport News, Va.*
Mechanics' Institute Library, *San Francisco, Calif.*
Mystic Seaport Museum, *Mystic, Conn.*
National Marine Historical Society, *Brooklyn, N.Y.*
National Maritime Museum, *Greenwich, England.*
National Maritime Museum, *San Francisco, Calif.*
New York Yacht Club, *New York, N.Y.*
Peabody Museum, *Salem, Mass.*
Nimitz Library, U.S. Naval Academy, *Annapolis, Md.*
Smithsonian Institution, *Washington, D.C.*
U.S. Coast Guard Academy, *New London, Conn.*
U.S. Naval Institute, *Annapolis, Md.*
U.S. Navy Museum, *Washington, D.C.*

Explanatory Notes

The Roman numeral after each definition denotes the century in which the term was first documented in English — Modern English being from the early sixteenth century; and Middle English, in which period a goodly number of terms appeared, from the eleventh to the early sixteenth. The small letters preceding the numerals indicate "early," "mid," "late," or "circa." The letters "p.e." after the numerals indicate "probably earlier," often implied by the word and meaning from which the term came.

You will note that many terms throughout the book are dated "e. XVII p.e." This is because very little was written on everyday maritime matters, especially to do with ships and their operation, before the XVII century. Two important writers were published at that time: the renowned Captain John Smith in 1627, and Sir Henry Manwayring (whose name is also seen as Mainwaring) whose work was written in 1623 and published in 1644. Both included texts of instruction in seamanship and glossaries of shipboard terms, many of which are included in this work.

Many mariners' terms came from words with other meanings as well, such as "arm," "back," "beam," etc. Sometimes a word's origin as a nautical term is unclear, whereas the word itself has a clear lineage that is, however, of little relevance to this work.

In many cases in which origins are from languages other than Modern English (and, as touched on, even in early Modern English), the spellings and meanings of some of the source words may not be totally accurate. I doubt if they ever can be; again, it is educated guessing. In the text I cite some of the early spellings. Also, an appendix contains a partial list of seventeenth-century spellings from Smith and Manwayring of terms in regular use today.

In citing sources, coded abbreviations have been used in order to conserve space in the text of the dictionary without compromising bibliographic precision. The capital letter-arabic numeral combinations appearing at the end of each dictionary entry refer to the user to the "Bibliography" section on page 202, where the codes along with their citations are displayed in alphabetical order.

Language Periods

The following is an alphabetical list of the languages cited in the text and their approximate time periods.

Anglo-French	1066–1200
Anglo-Latin	400–1300
Anglo-Norman	(see Anglo-French)
Anglo-Saxon	450–1150*
Early Modern English	1500–1700
Late Latin	300–700
Middle Dutch	1300–1500
Middle English	1150–1500
Middle Fresian	1300–1500
Old Dutch	Before 1300
Old English	450–1150*
Old French	800–1300
Old Icelandic	400–1500
Old Latin	7th to 1st centuries B.C. [700–100 B.C.?]
Old Norse	400–1500
Old Saxon	Before 1100
Other Ages;	
Egyptian	3500–1200 B.C.
Phoenician	1500–700 B.C.
Greek	1000–100 B.C.
Roman	500 B.C.–500 A.D.
Viking	700–1100 A.D.

*Anglo-Saxon and Old English are to some scholars the same, to others not so. Some use one, others use the other, and yet others (to clarify matters) use both. The time difference is inconsequential, so I have used both, quoting the authority I used.

Nautical Alphabet

This nautical alphabet is derived from the International Flag and Pennant Code.

Q 

R 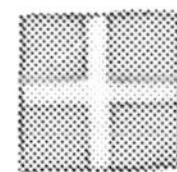

A 

I 

S 

B 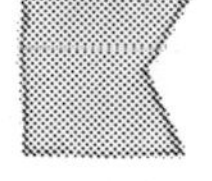

J 

T 

C 

K 

U 

D 

L 

V 

E 

M 

W 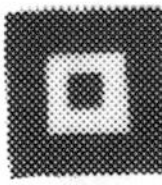

F 

N 

X 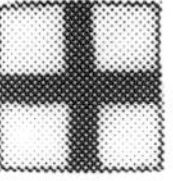

G 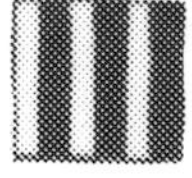

O 

Y 

H 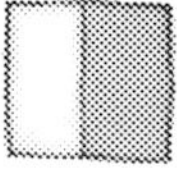

P 

Z 

A- A prefix, applying to many terms, as aback, abeam, aloft, etc.; meaning briefly, on, at, or in-the-state-of. (XII) It came into Early English from Anglo-Saxon, thence from Latin and Greek. WO-1, DE-3

A-1 This was Lloyd's early-days' best rating of a ship for insurance purposes. The letter pertained to the condition of the hull, and the numeral to her rigging and gear. Lloyd's classifications were initiated in 1756, and made law by the British Marine Act of 1876, having become a world standard in 1833. DE-1, K-1

A.B. Able-bodied seaman. (XVIII p.e.) A merchant seaman's rating, made legal and requirements standardized in Britain in 1894, and in the U.S., under the Seaman's Act of 1915 and now administered by the Coast Guard. DE-1, K-1

Aback Sail or sails backwinded. (XII) The word came from Old Norse — same word, same meaning. WO-1, WS-1

Abaft Aft of. (XII) This term comes from the Anglo-Saxon *beaften*, behind. WO-1, WS-1

Abeam At right angles to the fore-and-aft, or centerline, of a vessel. (XVI) It is from Anglo-Saxon. (See ***Beam***) S-1, WO-1

Aboard On or in a vessel. (XIV) As it has two sources, one Latin (***bordure***) and the other Anglo-Saxon (***bord***), both meaning side, this word suggests the wonderful wanderings of early navigators, such as the Danes to Greek shores, and the Romans to the Baltic, Northern Europe, and the British Isles. WO-1, DE-4

A-Burton Stowage of casks with their axes athwartships. (XIX p.e.) Probably so-called as applying particularly to stores readily accessible by deck tackle, i.e. a burton, at sea. S-2, S-3, C-1

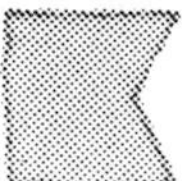

Admiral (1) Highest ranking officer in most navies. (XII-XIII) This word comes to us from the Arabic *amir-al-baka*, prince of the sea; via Latin and early French. WO-1, WS-1. (2) A very large fid, usually used by riggers. (p. XVIII) D-3, M-1, WO-1

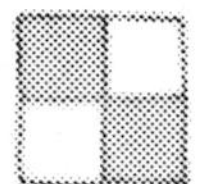

Advance The distance ahead on her old course that a vessel moves when making a turn. (See *Transfer*) The word comes from Latin, *ante*, then French, *avant*, and into English in the XVI century. When it came into mariners' use is not clear, although it was in such use in the XVII century. K-2, DE-3

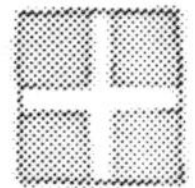

Adze Long-handled cutting tool, the blade of which is at right angles to the haft. (XIII) It was originally a ship-building tool, possibly as early as the V century by the Vikings. The word came to us from the Anglo-Saxon *adesa*, of the same meaning. WS-1, WW-1

Afloat The desirable condition of floating. (XII) Another word of Anglo-Saxon origin, *floetan*. WS-1, WW-1

Aft An adverb, meaning toward the stern. (Possibly XV) Yet another word from Anglo-Saxon, *aeft*, rear, back it also entered Dutch and German with the same meaning. WO-1, WS-1

After An adjective, meaning toward the stern. (XVI) It comes from Anglo-Saxon, *aefter*, toward the rear. (The word is often, and not quite correctly, contracted to "aft".) WO 1

After-Guard is an ever changing word in meaning. In the XVII and XVIII centuries, it referred to a ship's officers, who always worked and lived in the after-area of a vessel (and referred to by one writer as "poop people"). In the late XIX and early XX centuries it denoted the owner's party on yachts, most of which had at least some paid crews. In this sense it has come to mean the crew leaders in larger racing yachts, such as the America's Cup contenders. B-6, K-1, DE-3

Agonic Line A line of points on a chart at which there is no magnetic compass variation. The word comes from the Greek *agonos*, meaning no angle. (l. XVIII) DE-5

Ahoy The traditional hailing call. (Possibly XIII) *Hoi* is still the blind-corner signal of Venetian gondoliers, apparently having come into use in the early days of these craft. It was once the dreaded battle cry of the Vikings, and appears in Middle English and Old French. L-8, WS-1

A-Hull Under "bare poles." (Probably XVI) An old term for running with no sail, as in a storm, was the word "hulling." The newer term became better known to some with the problems of the 1979 Fastnet Race. WS-1, DE-3

Aldis Lamp A hand-held spotlight with a trigger-like switch, for signalling. (e. XX) Aldis is believed to be a trade name. JR

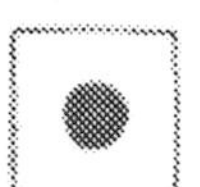

Alee To leeward. (XIV) (See *Lee*) Similar words appear in the Scandinavian languages and in Dutch. WO-1, DE-5

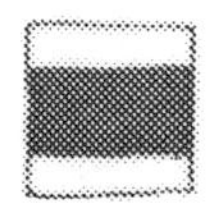

Alidade An instrument for taking bearings. (XV) This term came, through Middle English and Latin, from the Arabic word *albidadah*, for turning radius. B-1, DE-5

All-a-Taut (also *All-Taut*) Everything ready-to-go, shipshape and in good order for putting to sea (or for inspection). The saying is believed to be a U.S.N. colloquialism, probably from the early XIX. N-4, WP-1C

Alley (also *Alleyway*) A shipboard passageway. (XIV) The word comes from the Old French *alée*, probably of the same meaning. It later was also the term for the passageway on a galley. WO-1

All Hands and the Cook is a phrase around which there could be some debate. (XIX) It was the battle cry for a cowpuncher crew in the West when moving cattle under difficult conditions, but in our world it was the order on a Grand Banks schooner when everyone turned out. ("When the cook came on deck," said one Nova Scotian, "we did have problems!") H-2

Aloft Up a mast. (XII) This word is one of surprisingly few that seems to have originated in English. WO-1

Alow A word now rarely heard, meaning on deck, vis-a-vis aloft. (XIII) WO-1

A-Main An old term, still occasionally heard in Britain, for "all-at-once" or "on the run." (XVI) It comes from the Anglo-Saxon *maegen*, force, power. W-2, WO-1

Amidships In the center of a vessel, or on her centerline. (XVII p.e.) The word came from both German and Dutch — it is not known which came first. The latter was *midscheeps*, of this meaning. WO-1

Anchor A device for mooring a floating object to the bottom. Here's one for you! Clearly traceable from the Greek — *agkura* — possibly from the X century B.C., it is believed to have come to that language from the Phoenicians at least 500 years before. From the Greek, it can be traced, through Latin and the older European languages, to Middle and Modern English. The word can be recognized in virtually all European languages, including Russian (*yakor'*). One scholar suggests that the word is related to *ankh*, the Egyptian cross, but this is very doubtful as most anchors in those days were simply weights or in the form of a simple hook. W-2, WO-1

Anchor Watch Crew members standing watch while a vessel is moored. (XVII p.e.) Captain John Smith wrote, "lest some miscreants from ye shippes about should steal ye anchors or other gear whilste they, the crew, sleepeth." S-2

Anemometer A device for measuring wind velocity. (XIX) The term comes from the Greek words *anem*, wind, and *metron*, measure. DE-5

Annie Oakley is the nickname of an early parachute spinnaker for racing sailboats, that had a series of holes on its center seam. (XX) It was named for the famous markslady of Buffalo Bill's Wild West Shows. B-6, R-2

Annunciator A device for transmitting orders from the bridge of a ship to the engine room, generally for the main engine(s). (XIX) The word was created from the Latin *annutilatus*, announce. DE-5

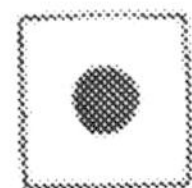

Antipodean Day The day gained (or lost) crossing the International Dateline (approximately the 180th meridian) heading west. (XVII p.e.) The word comes from the Greek *hoi antipodes*, roughly meaning opposite. B-6, DE-5

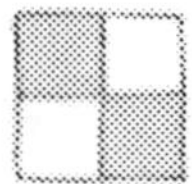

Aplusier (also *Aplustre*) An ornament on a vessel's stern, also an old term for a bas-relief nameboard on the transom. (XVIII p.) The term probably came from Greek and to us from Latin. DE-3

Apostles An old nickname for knights, large single bitts on the deck of an older square-rigger. (l. XVII p.e.) It is a good guess that the term — typical of sailors' invention — came from the fact that there usually were twelve of them. L-4, WAB

Apparel An old term, though sometimes still heard, for all the removable gear on a vessel. (Probably VII) The word comes from the Old French *apareille*, meaning equipment, and probably was a sailor's term meaning to make fit, or to fit out a vessel. B-1, WO-1

Ardent Another old term, meaning to have a weather helm. (XIV) The word comes from Latin, *ardens*, but whether in this sense is not certain. F-1b, WO-1

Arm To the mariner, this is a verb, to put tallow into the cavity of the hand lead, to get samples of the bottom when sounding. (XII) The term comes from the French *armer*, meaning to equip. K-1, DE-4

Armada A fleet of ships. (XVI) Its origin is the Latin *armator*, meaning any armed force. At the time when the term was in use, virtually all offshore vessels had some kind of armament. WO-1

Arrive Hardly a sea term, but it once was. (XVI) It came from French, in turn from the Latin word *arripare*, of which the meaning, and the early English one too, was to land, or to come ashore. WW-1

Arse An old term for the fall-side of a block; also called the choke. (e. XVII p.e.) The word could go back to the Greek *orsa*, tail. B-1, DE-3

Articles The short name for Shipping Articles, the master contract between the members of the crew — usually everyone but the master — and the owners. (XVIII) Such a document hs been required on American merchant vessels from the late XIX century. DE-1, DE-4

Asdic The early name for underwater search and detection equipment for submarines, by echo ranging. It is an acronym for Anti-Submarine Detection Investigation Committee, a joint British and French project started at the end of World War I. (See *Sonar*) K-1

Ash Breeze Becalmed. (Probably XVII) Under this condition a ship's boats were put out, to tow her by rowing. The term may have been in use earlier, applying to smaller sailing vessels that could use oars. B-6, H-1

Ashore On shore. (XVI) An earlier term was a-land. WO-1

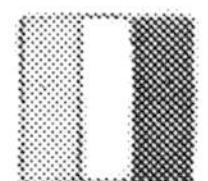

Astrolabe A predecessor to the sextant; an instrument for measuring the altitude of celestial bodies. (XVII) The term comes to us via French and Latin, from the Greek word *astrolabeon*, meaning star taking. WO-1

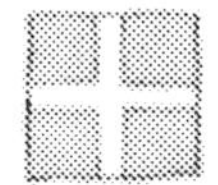

Athwartships Across a vessel or boat. (XIV) This word comes from an old Icelandic one, *þwert*, of this same meaning. WO-1, WS-1

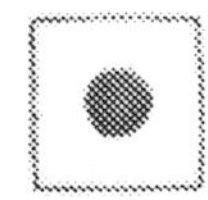

A-Trip Said of the anchor when it has broken ground on being hoisted. (e. XVII p.e.) (See *Aweigh*) It probably came either from Old French, *treper*, or Old English, *treppan*, one meaning of which was in motion. S-2, WO-1

A-Try To lay hove-to. (XVII p.e.) (See *Try*) DE-3

Avast A shipboard order, to hold, or stop hauling. (e. XVII p.e.) This term appears to come from Old Dutch (*hou'vest*), and could be related to the Portuguese word *abasta*, enough, and could go back to Arabic. S-2, WW-1

Awash Said when the decks are at or near waterlevel or inundated with water. (XV) It came from Old English (*waesan*) thence from Old Norse and Old Saxon. A similar word exists in the modern Nordic languages. WO-1

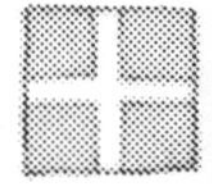

Aweigh Said of the anchor when it is off the bottom when hoisting. (Possibly XV) (See *Atrip*) Weigh in this sense seems to be derived from the Old Icelandic word *vega*, meaning to lift, or carry. S-1, WO-1

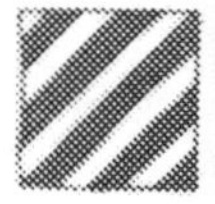

Awning Shade over a deck, deck opening, or for a boat. (e. XVII p.e.) The origin appears to be Old French, *auvan*, which meant a shade over a ship's deck. M-2, DE-3

Aye (also *Aye-Aye*) The sailor's way of saying "yes," or "I understand." (XVI) In common use in English ashore as well as aboard ship in the XVI century, it has two possible sources; one, the Old French *je* or *o je* (yes, that say I); and the other, the more likely early English *yie*, yes. WO-1, DE-5

Azimuth The bearing, or horizontal direction, of a celestial body. (e. XVII p.e.) The term probably comes from the Arabic *assamut*, for points on the horizon. WS-1, DE-5

Back (1) Said of the wind, to change direction clockwise or to leeward. (2) Said of a sail, to move it to bring the wind on its reverse side. (3) (See *Backbone*) In all senses, (XIV) The origin is Anglo-Saxon, ***bac***. S-1, WS-1

Back and Fill A method for a sailing ship to maneuver using her sails to control forward motion, i.e., filling and backing her sails. (e. XVII p.e.) M-2

Backbone The main fore-and-aft lower structural members of the hull. (XVI) DE-3

Backstay Any of a variety of stays leading aft from a mast to the deck. (XVII) Thought of, perhaps, as a relatively modern element of rigging, this obviously is not the case. A-2, DE-3

Baggywrinkle (also ***Bagawringle, Bangawrinkle, Baggywringle, etc.,***) Padding to inhibit chafe aloft. (Probably e. XIX) The origins of both the device and the term are uncertain; also uncertain is whether the term is American, British, or Canadian. Our guess is the ***baggy*** means what it says, ***wringle*** is an Old English word for wrap or twist, and wrinkle is a corruption. (It is also known as railway sennit.) A-2, DE-3

Bagpiping Sheeting a sail to bring it aback, particularly the mizzen of a square-rigger. (XVIII) The origin is uncertain but it probably pertains to the bag-like curves of a sail when aback. L-4, S-3

Bail To dip out water. (XVII) The word is derived from Late Latin, ***bacula***, pail, and came to us from Old French, ***bail***, bucket. DE-3

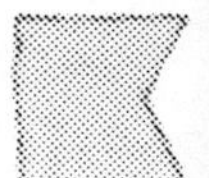

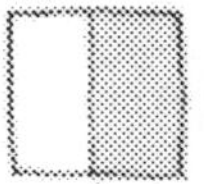

Baldheaded Rig Said of a gaff-rigged schooner with no topmasts. The term in all likelihood originated in the Northeast, referring to fishing schooners so rigged or with the topmasts sent down for winter weather; it became more common with the advent of motor power. C-1a, WAB

Bale A curved hoop or band, of several uses; on a block, track, or on deck. (e. XVII p.e.) The term possibly came from the Old Norse *beyzja*, to bend. It was sometimes spelled *bail*, which no doubt created some confusion for the few mariners who could spell at all. S-2, DE-5

Ballast Weight to provide or improve a vessel's stability. (e. XVII p.e.) The origin is probably Old Danish, *barlast*, bare load. S-2, WS-1

Bar (1) A bank or shoal. (XVI) This comes from Old French, *barre,* of this meaning. (2) Unit of atmospheric pressure in the metric system. In this sense the word comes from the Greek *baros*, pressure. B-6, WS-1

Barber Hauler A line to control the angle or lead of a jib sheet. (XX) A very modern term, named for its inventor, Merrit Barber, a well-known racing skipper. R-3

Barge (1) A powerless vessel for hauling cargo. (2) Formerly a highly ornamented ceremonial craft. No doubt this is the reason why this is what a navy ship's or shore-station boat is called when it is assigned to an admiral. (XIII) The word came from the Greek *baris*, for Egyptian boat, and to us from the Latin *barca*, barge. N-4, WO-1, WS-1

Bark (also ***Barque***) A sailing vessel of three or more masts, all but the aftermost square-rigged, it being fore-and-aft. Vessels of this definition were seen in the XIX (p.e.). Earlier (XVIII) bark meant a hull form rather than a rig, with little or no head-structure at the bow, and a square stern; it could be any rig. The word is from the French ***barque***, which is from Portuguese and Latin (***barica***). W-2, WO-1, WS-1, WAB

Barkentine A vessel similar to a bark, except that only the foremast is square-rigged. The term has the same basic origin as ***Bark***. WO-1

Barometer An instrument for measuring atmospheric pressure. Invented by Galileo, it was first used in weather studies in the XVIIth century, the aneroid barometer coming into practical use in the late XVIIIth. The term is based on the Greek word for pressure, ***baros***. DE-1, DE-5

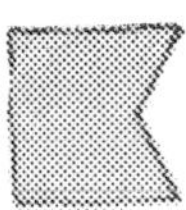

Barratry Broadly, an illegal act or breach of trust by a ship's master. (XVII) The word comes, via Middle English, from the French ***barratarie***, fraud. WO-1

Bateau The French word for boat, this generally refers in North America to flat-bottomed, oar-propelled craft of the XVIII and early XIX. They were double-ended, with a sharp and raked bow and stern and much sheer, and were used on the rivers and lakes of the Northeast and what we now call the northeast part of the Middle West. The word itself originally may have gone to France from England (Old English). WO-1, D-3, JG, WAB

Battens (1) Heavy timbers used to cover cargo hatches. (2) Shaped boards or strips of plastic used to improve the set of fore-and-aft sails. (XVII, for the first sense.) The word comes to us from Old French, ***baston***, strip or stick of wood. S-2, WO-1

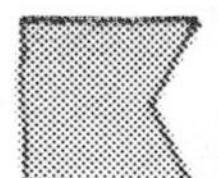

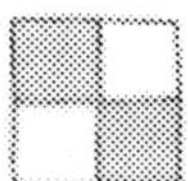

Baulk A heavy piece of timber, also an old term for deckbeam. (possibly XII) The term may have come from the Old English word *balca*, ridge. Another possibility for it may be a corruption of Baltic, as much timber for ships came from that area. (Baulking is still a Down-Easter's term for hauling heavy or long timbers or spars.) S-2, JR

Bay Shipboard space or section. (XIV) The word comes from the Old French *baie*, to stand open. WO-1

Beach The seaman's meaning is "any shore." (XVI) WS-1, N-4

Beacon A shoreside marker, to indicate a channel or a hazard. (e. XVII p.e.) Its origin is an Old English word, *beacn*, of about the XIIth century, and of this same meaning. S-2, WO-1

Beakhead Earlier, a ram on the bow of a fighting galley, later a platform forward of the stem for archers and musketmen. (XV) Still later, it was a smaller pointed platform with various uses. (See *Head*) The origin of the term is obscure, but the word got around — it appears to have come from Old French, *bec*, beak, this from Late Latin and this in turn from Gaulish. There also was a Celtic word *bec,* or *beq*. S-1, S-2, DE-3

Beam (1) The measure of breadth of a craft. S-1, WS-1 (2) A structural unit, particularly a deck beam. (XIII in both senses) The word is derived from the Anglo-Saxon *beam*, tree. S-1, WO-1

Bear (1) A term denoting the direction of an object from a vessel. (2) To sail (or steam) in an indicated direction. (e. XVII p.e.) The word came from the Old Norse *beran*, possibly in both senses. S-2, DE-3

Bear a Hand A sailor's order to "get moving," "tend to business," etc. The phrase was seen in the early XVIII; its origin is obscure. K-2, N-4

Bearding Angle The angle of the line of the stem or stern structure to the keel. (XVII) This term comes from the Middle English *berden*, bevelling. DE-3, DE-5

Bearing (See *Bear*)

Beat To sail to windward on successive tacks, or boards. (Probably XVIII) The origin in the nautical sense is uncertain, as is the time; the latter no doubt related to improvements of ship design and rigging, resulting in improved ability of ships to work to windward. (See *Tack*, Board) DE-5

Beaufort Scale A table of degrees of wind velocity, standard among mariners of many flags. It was first published in 1805 by a British admiral, Sir Francis Beaufort, a highly-regarded scholar of marine sciences. K-1

Becket A small loop of rope or small stuff, of many uses. (e. XVII p.e.) The origin is not known, but the word may have come from Old English, and earlier from Old Dutch, *bogt*, bend of rope. DE-3

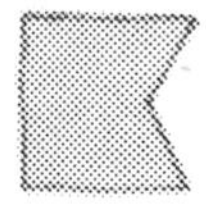

Becue To fasten a line to the crown of an anchor before lowering, to facilitate tripping it when ready to weigh. (Probably XVIII p.e.) The origin of this term is uncertain; it possibly is from the French *Queue*, and this from the Old French *coue*, for tail. DE-3, Conjecture

Bees Leads on the sides of the bowsprit, for foremast stays, on a square-rigger. (e. XVII p.e.) The word comes from Middle English, *beghe*, metal ring, possibly having a nautical sense. It in turn came from Old English. A-2, DE-4

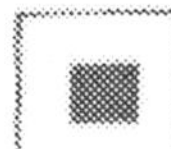

Beetle A large mallet, believed to have been originally a shipbuilder's and shipboard carpenter's tool. (Probably XV) Earlier sometimes spelled beatle, the term comes from the Anglo-Saxon word *betel*, mallet. (See *Commander*) WO-1

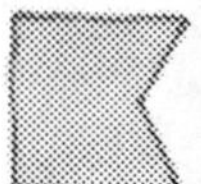

Belay To make fast, secure, tie, or stop. (XVI) Its derivation is Old English, *belecgam*, of these same meanings. WO-1, DE-5

Belaying Pin Wooden, and later metal, specially shaped bar, by which running rigging is belayed, or made fast. (It was also a wicked weapon in a fight or in the hand of one of the notorious "bullymates" of yesteryear.) The device was in common use in the early XVIII. A-2, WW-1

Bell, Ship's It is not known when ship's bells were first carried; it may have been in the XVI century. We do know that they were in use in the XVII in the same manner as is traditional now, to mark the time, particularly of the watches, of one to eight strokes for the four-hour period. (An interesting note: an old custom, still followed in some ships, is to strike sixteen bells at midnight on New Year's Eve.) (See *Watch*) L-1

Below Below decks, or down from aloft. (XVII) Scholars say the word was a "late bloomer" in the general language, seen in late Middle English. (See *Alow*) WO-1, DE-4

Bend As a noun, the product of fastening one rope's end to another. As a verb, doing the above, or fastening a line to a sail, the anchor, etc.; also the term used for rigging a sail. (e. XVII p.e.) It is derived from the Old English word *benden*, of the same meanings. S-2, DE-5

Bender Originally a mariner's word for a drinking party. (XVIII) The origin of the word is obscure; it is probably Scottish. M-1, DE-3

Bending Shot The first part of the anchor cable, whether rope or chain, which is bent to the anchor and usually heavier than the rest of the cable. (Possibly XVI) Shot is probably a corruption of *shoot*, an Old and Middle English word for splice. (See *Foreganger, Shot*) DE-3

Berm A narrow shoal or bank, or a raised embankment, along a river or shoreline. (XVI) The term comes from Old Norse, *barmr*, brim. D-3, WO-1

Bermuda (also *Bermudian)* One name for the sails and rig most commonly seen on sailing yachts today. (1. XIX) The sail shape is triangular, as were the sails of most sailing craft in Bermuda's waters; hence the name. K-1

Berth (1) Sea room, sufficient space to maneuver. (2) Living space assigned, or billet, on board. (3) A duty assignment, as for "the third mate's berth." (All these, XVIII p.e.) Earlier spellings were *birth* and *byrth*. The term comes from Old English, *besan*, of the same sense, at least of the first meaning. S-2, WO-1

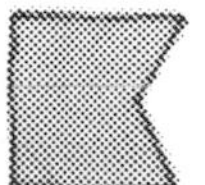

Between-Decks (See *'Tween-Decks*)

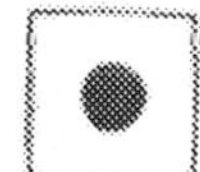

Bibbs (also *Bibs)* Heavy brackets on a mast, to support the trestle trees. (e. XVII p.e.) The origin of the word in this sense is not known. A-2

Bilge (1) The underwater transverse ('thwartship) curve, or outer shape of the hull. (XV) The earlier word in English was *billage*; its origin was the French word *bouge*, bulge. (2) The lower part of the interior of the hull, usually below the floors. (XV) It was also seen earlier as billage, and probably has the same origin. (See *Floors*) S-1, WO-1

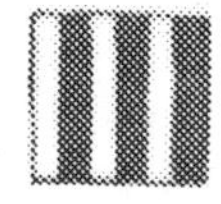

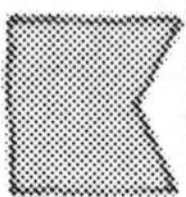

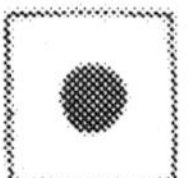

Bill (1) A general term for a document or notice, such as a waybill, bill of lading, or watch bill. (XVI) The word comes from the Late Latin *billa*, of the same meaning. (2) One name for the tip of an anchor-fluke. (Possibly XI) The origin in this sense is uncertain, but it could be Middle English (*bile*) for a bird's beak. K-1, DE-3

Billboard An angled plate at the rail forward, for housing an anchor. (m. XIX) The term's origin is obscure; it could relate to that part of an anchor often called the bill. K-2, DE-5

Billet A berth or duty assignment, usually on a military ship. (XVIII p.e.) The origin is Middle French, *billette*, and it came through Middle English, *bylet*, probably a soldier's term. WO-1, WS-1

Billet head A relatively simple scrollwork ornament at a ship's bow. Also, the term was used for a specially-constructed stempiece of a whaleboat. (e. XIX) The word is believed to be of Celtic origin, to have come back to English from Old French *billete*. C-1g, DE-5

Billy Generally a Scottish term, but sometimes heard in this country, for a variety of light machines, tools, and other gear. (XVIII) It is probably of Celtic origin. (See *Handy Billy*) WO-1

Binnacle The stand on which a compass is mounted. (XV) The earlier word was *bittacle*. The term came from the French *habitacle*, and that from the Latin *habitaculum*, a place of habitation. Before the days of the compass, it was used for a lamp or lantern. The word binnacle appeared in the XVIII. S-2, WO-1

Binnacle List A ship's sick-list. In the XVIII century and probably before, a list was given to the officer or mate of the watch, containing the names of men unable to report for duty. The list was kept at the binnacle. D-3, N-4

Binocular Double telescope. While not originally a mariner's instrument, it is now, of course, and one of his most useful. First conceived of by the Dutch in the XVI century, it came into general use in the XIX. The word is adapted from the Latin *bini*, two together, and *oculus*, eye. WO-1

Bitt A strong vertical structural timber or metal post, used to make fast heavy lines; usually in pairs, ergo bitts. (XIV) The term came from Dutch, *beting*, and this from Old Norse, *biti*, crossbeam. It is related to the Late Latin word *bitus*, whipping post. WO-1

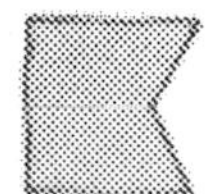

Bitter-End The inboard end of a line, especially a mooring line or the anchor cable or chain. The earlier term was bitters-end. Quoting Captain John Smith (1627), "the part of the cable that doth stay within board, the bitter being that part actually on the bitts." (XV p.e.) (See *Bitt*) S-2, WO-1

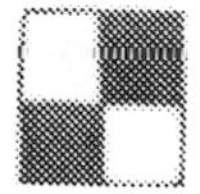

Black Down, To (1) Tarring standing rigging in the days of rope. (2) The practice, for British naval vessels, and possibly American, in the XVIII and early XIX centuries, of blackening their topsides, usually as a disguise. S-3

Black-Gang Now the engineer's section of a crew (and in modern machinery spaces, occasions are rarer when one gets very dirty any more). It referred originally to the boiler-room crew in early coal-burning steamships. It hardly needs further comment. DE-5

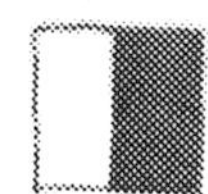

Block is the shipboard term for that all-important device known ashore as the pulley, and has an almost countless variety of types, sizes, and uses. (XIV) The origin of the word is the Old French *bloc*, of the same meaning. Similar words also were seen in Early Dutch and German. WO-1, DE-5

Bluejacket One of several nicknames for naval enlisted men, both U.S. and British. The term came into being shortly after navy sailors began to wear real uniforms, which included, obviously, a (short) blue jacket. (e. XVIII) K-1, WO-1

Bluenose is the name given to men and vessels of Nova Scotia. (e. XVIII) There are two possible origins, of which I prefer the first, which is the obvious effect of the weather in that part of the world. The other is that both are named for the Nova Scotia Bluenose potato, which is considered by some to be the best there is. WM-1, JR

Blue Peter The merchant mariner's name for the International Signal Code "P" flag, which, when flown from the signal mast, indicates that the ship will sail that day. Probably first used by the British Navy in the early XVII, it was a recall to the crew, "that they shall repair on board," and for shoresiders to conclude whatever business they had with the vessel. It is not certain where the name came from, but it is a good guess that Peter is a corruption of repeater, the flag having been used also to request that a flag signal on another ship be repeated. (It is a blue flag with a white rectangle in its center.) K-1, DE-3

Blue Ribbon (also *Blue Riband*) The reward for the ship, then always a passenger liner, that held the transatlantic crossing record, from about 1840. Several British ships held it, also French and German. The first and last American were the SS *Baltic* in 1852, and the *United States*, the latter with an average speed of nearly thirty-six knots, for about three days and ten hours, in 1952. K-1

Board (1) A tack, or "leg," sailing to windward; an old term still sometimes used referring to square-riggers. (XIV) Its derivation is obscure in this sense. (2) To go aboard any craft. (XV) The word has several sources, including Anglo-Saxon *bord*, for side. (See *Aboard*) S-1, WS-1

Boat A general term for any small craft; also used until recently by submariners for their craft. (XIII) The word comes from Old Norse, from two possible source-words, *beit* and *bato*. Similar words appear today in all the Nordic languages and in French. S-1, WO-1, DE-3

Landsmen often ask, "when do you say boat and when ship?" A captain I knew used to tell his passengers, "think in the terms of fleas and their dog."

Boatswain The leading petty officer of the deck crew of a merchant ship, also a warrant officer of the deck force in the Navy and Coast Guard, petty officers of this specialty in these services being boatswain's mates. (XV p.e.) The word is pronounced bos'n; it is one of the few that originated in English. *Swain* meant attendant or assistant, and comes from Old English, *swan*, of the same sense. DE-3, WO-1

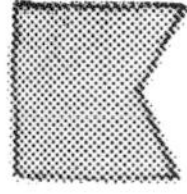

Boatswain's Pipe (also *Boatswain's Call*) A whistle of peculiar shape and shrill tone, used by boatswains and their mates in the Sea Services to signal various routine orders; so used since the XVIII. Up to the mid-XVII, it often was made of precious metal and sometimes bejewelled, was worn on a gold or silver chain, and was a badge of office of high ranking maritime dignitaries. S-2

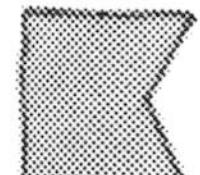

Bobstay A heavy stay rigged from the bowsprit tip to the stem. (XVI) The derivation of bob is uncertain, but it probably comes from a Celtic word meaning short. A-2, DE-3

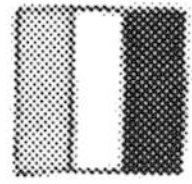

Bollard A strong vertical post to which hawsers are secured, both aboard ship and shoreside. (XIV) The term in all likelihood came from an Old Norse word *bols*, tree trunk. WO-1

Bollocks (also *Bullock Blocks*) Blocks on the topmast of a square-rigger, through which the topsail tyes are rove. (e. XVII p.e.) The origin of the term is not known. S-2

Bolster A shaped and smooth piece of softwood on the trestletrees of a square-rigger's mast, to impede chafe. Also the rounded "lip" on a hawsehole or fairlead, for the same purpose. (XVI) Its origin is the Old Norse *bolstr*, pad. A-2, WW-1

Boltrope The binding line around the edges of a sail, awning, or cover. (XIV) It is derived from the Old German word *bolz*, meaning rope. S-1

Bonaventure A lateen sail on its own (fourth) mast, way aft; in use on galleons of the XVI and XVII centuries. It may have been named for a vessel owned by England's Queen Elizabeth I, the *Elizabeth Bonaventure*, or possibly because many ships carried a trading document so named in that period.

The mast was called the bonaventure mizzen, and often was adorned with pennants and flags. As such it may well have been the predecessor of the stern (ensign) staff. K-1

Bonnet An extra piece of sail attached to the foot of a square sail or to the leach of a fore-and-aft sail, for added sail area in mild weather. (XIV) The term comes from the French word *bonet*, of the same meaning. S-1, S-2, DE-3

Boom The lower spar of a fore-and-aft sail, a spar on which a studding sail was set on a square-rigger; also a type of shipboard crane for handling cargo and supplies. The word was seen in the XVI century, but was used more commonly from the XVIII, when fore-and-aft sails were replacing lateen. It probably came from the Old Norse word ***bathum***, meaning beam. WO-1

Boot The nickname for a Navy or Coast Guard recruit. The term became general in Navy slang about the time of World War I, I am told; but it is believed to have gotten started about the turn of the century, when recruits eschewed scrubbing decks in the then-traditional barefoot manner, and wore seaboots. Unlike today, it was then considered a term of disdain, and, it is said, often used with an inelegant adjective. WM-3a

Bootlegger An old term for smuggler, revived in Prohibition days. (probably e. XVIII) Sailors smuggling goods ashore hid them in their seaboots. WO-1, Pub-3

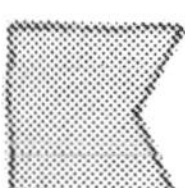

Boot Top The painted band on a boat or ship, from just above to slightly below the waterline. (c. XVIII p.e.) Boot-topping, now the paint used and the process itself, was an earlier term for coating the entire bottom. F-1b, DE-3

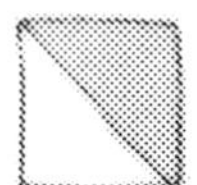

Bore Sudden strong tide wave or surge, most often occurring on the northeastern shores of the North Atlantic. (XIV) The word came, via Middle English, either from Old Norse or Icelandic, possibly both. The old word in both languages was ***bara***, of the same meaning. WO-1

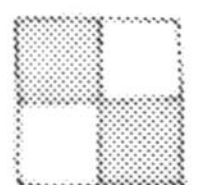

Bottom hardly needs definition. In the sense of referring to ships, it was seen in the XIII, and came from the Anglo-Saxon word ***botm***. S-1, WO-1

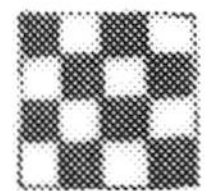

Bound Said of a vessel as to her destination. (XIII) It stems from the Old Norse word ***bounded,*** destined. WO-1

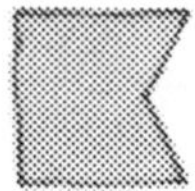

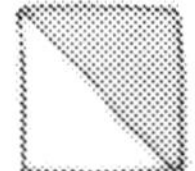

Bow The forward end of any craft. Also the *bows*, i.e., the sides at the bow. (XV) The word probably comes from Old Icelandic, *bogr*, meaning shoulder. Related words are seen in all the old, and some of the modern Nordic languages. S-1, WO-1

Bowditch A household word among navigators, a textbook filled with tabular data most helpful in their work. Nathaniel Bowditch was one of this country's, if not the world's, most renowned mariner-mathematicians. His first book, *The American Practical Navigator*, was first published in 1802, and has been perpetuated by the Navy since 1866. DE-1

Bower An anchor routinely used when anchoring. (e. XVII p.e.) The word simply comes from the fact that such anchors were carried at the bows. F-1b, WO-1

Bowline (1) One of a sailor's most useful knots. (2) A line or tackle for trimming the foresail of a square-rigger. (IX) The term appears to have come at us from two directions; Icelandic *bogr*, bow, and Old French *boeline*, sounding line. S-2, WO-1

Bowse An old term meaning to haul or to heave, generally downwards. (e. XVII p.e.) The derivation is obscure. Etymologists mention the term, but only in relation to tippling. (Is there some connection?) S-2

Bowsprit The spar in the stem of a vessel to which the headsails are fastened and the foremast stayed. (XIII) The Dutch were using them before the British, so naturally enough, the term came from Holland, *boegspriet*. (See *Widowmaker*) S-1, WW-1

Box A verb, to name the points of the compass. The term probably evolved in the XVIII century, and, again probably, came from the Spanish *bajar*, to sail around. WO-1

Boxhaul (also *Box Haul*) To wear ship in a square-rigger, in limited space, sometimes to minimize forward movement. Its origin is uncertain, but in all probability is the same as for *Box*. WO-1

Braces Lines, usually with tackles, from the ends of the yards to the deck of a square-rigger. (e. XVII p.e.) The term comes from Old French, ***bras***, arm, could relate to Latin and go back to Greek, ***brachion***, arm. S-2

Brail Both noun and verb, relates to a line used to gather in a sail. (XV) Earlier spelled brale, it came from Old French, ***braile***, belt. S-1, WO-1

Brass Monkey The nickname for the famed Cunard Line's houseflag, a gold lion rampant on a red field. (1. XIX) Pub-2, JR

Brass Pounder Another nickname, this one for early-day radio operators, whose transmitter keys were made of brass. (e. XX) JR

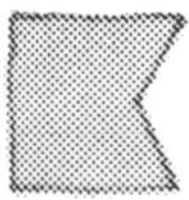

Breach A large wave that breaks across the deck of a vessel. (XIII) It is derived from the Old French word ***breche***, meaning break. DE-5

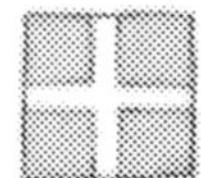

Break Out To put something to use, such as food or gear from the storerooms or hold, or a flag or a sail that has been in stops; also said of freeing an anchor from the bottom. (e. XVIII p.e.) The term's origin is Old English, ***brecan***, one meaning of which is to break open. F-1b, WS-1

Breaker (1) A wave that breaks, particularly over rocks or a shoal. The word comes from Anglo-Saxon, ***breken***, of this same meaning. (XV) (2) A small cask. (XIX p.e.) This word comes from the Spanish ***bareca***, barrel. WO-1

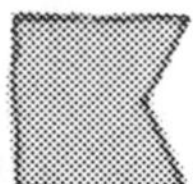

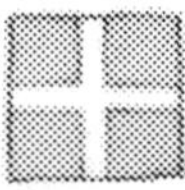

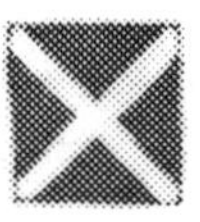

Bream An old term for cleaning a vessel's bottom, earlier with furze, later with torches. (e. XVII p.e.) Its origin is probably Danish, *bram*, furze. (Furze is another name for gorse.) M-2, WW-1

Breast (1) A verb, implying abeam; i.e., to breast-off is fend off or push away, and to breast-in is the reverse. (XIV) (2) As a noun, a mooring line leading approximately abeam. (XVII p.e.) An earlier term was breast-fast. The origin of the term in both senses is Old Norse, *brjost*. Its earlier English spelling was sometimes brest. S-2, DE-5

Breasthook A horizontal, angled brace in the bow of any craft. (XVII p.e.) Its origin is the same as for breast. S-1

Breech Said of a block, the part opposite the swallow; the fall side. It is also called the arse or the choke. (XVII p.e.) The origin of the term in this sense is not known. (See *Arse*.) M-2, DE-5

Breeches Buoy A life-ring with a canvas seat that looks like a pair of breeches or pants. It is fitted with a harness by which it can be hauled along a "trolley line," for rescue purposes. It was a British invention, adopted by the U.S. Life-Saving Service, first mentioned in its manual dated 1876. USCG

Breeze A light wind. This word demonstrates how meanings can change over the years. It was in use in the XVII century in its present meaning, but the earlier English word is believed to mean a heavy wind, as does the French word from which it is derived, *brize*. S-2, WS-1

Bridge The control center of a power vessel. The early bridge (mid-XIX) was an elevated 'thwartship platform, usually betwen or just forward of the paddle-boxes of a sidewheeler, and was structured like a shore-side light footbridge. Despite many changes in shape and size over the years, the name has stuck. K-1, JR

Bridle Any of many arrangements of line, chain, etc., of two or more parts. Such gear having so many applications it is hard to know when the word came into use on the water, but it was seen in the XVII, and the word came for Old English, ***bridel***, braid. S-2, WO-1

Brig (1) Now the best known definition is a square-rigged vessel of two masts, square-rigged on both. (e. XVIII) (See *Brigantine, Snow*). WO-1, WAB (2) A naval jail. The origin in this sense appears to be that old stripped-down ships, often two-masted, were used for this purpose. (XVIII p.e.)

The definitions of the brig and brigantine appear to have varied with the times. One of these, dated 1801, described a brig as what not long after was to be called a brigantine. WO-1, WAB

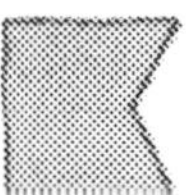

Brigantine Earlier (XVI) any vessel used by the brigands of the French coast and of the West Indies, of any rig. The term came to mean a two-masted vessel with a square-rigged foremast and a mainsail that could be square or fore-and-aft rigged. (l. XVII)

Later, (e. XVIII) the square-rigged foremast and the fore-and-aft main with square topsails became characteristic. Still later, a strictly fore-and-aft main became fixed for definitive purposes. (See *Brig, Hermaphrodite Brig*) There no doubt was some confusion in defining the rig, as one authority tells us that cusom house clerks often wrote up brigantine as brig[a] or as brig, thence in good probability the origin of this latter term. WO-1, DE-5, WAB

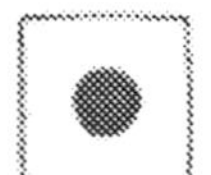

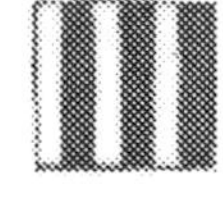

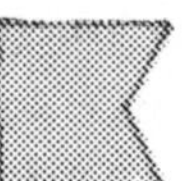

Brightwork Varnished woodwork, especially topside. (XIX p.e.) Bright it should be and work it is. The term has degenerated in some circles to refer to metal as well, which is kept polished. B-6, WS-1

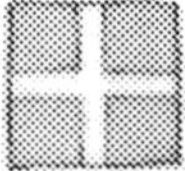

Bristol Fashion Neat, clean, and in good condition—in a word, "shipshape." (XVI) The phrase stems from the days when Bristol was a bustling port, and ships from there were renowned for this characteristic. D-1, K-1

Broach (also *Broach To*) What a sailing craft does when she unvoluntarily turns too much to windward when running free. (e. XVIII p.e.) The origin of the term is not certain, but it appears to be Old French, ***brochier***, thence to French and then to Middle English, ***brochen***. The meaning of both words was turn. DE-3

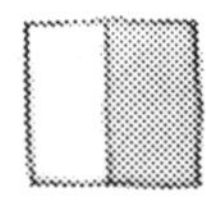

Broad refers to bearings, i.e., "broad on the bow," or "broad abeam"—45° and 90° respectively. (e. XVII p.e.) It comes from the Anglo-Saxon word ***brad***, meaning wide. WS-1

Broadside The side of a vessel; also the firing of the "main battery" on one side of a warship. (XVII) The origin is the same as for broad. S-2

Brow A light-weight gangplank. (XVII p.e.) Its direct origin is believed to be Danish or Swedish, both ***bro***, bridge. Its earlier derivation was Old English, ***bryeg***, bridge. S-2, DE-3

Brummel Hook A patented and special sister-hook used on modern sailboats. (1. XX) It is believed to be a trade name. R-3

Buccaneer A Spanish Main pirate of the XVII and XVIII centuries. The term comes from the French ***boucanier***, pirate or hunter. WO-1

Buckler A plate or shield over a hawsehole or hawse pipe, to keep water from washing aboard. (XVI) The term no doubt is after that for a small armor-shield when armor was worn, and comes from Middle English. DE-5, JR

Bugeye A double-ended, shoal-draft, ketch-rigged vessel with extreme-raked masts, characteristic of Chesapeake Bay. (m. XIX p.e.) While these vessels were registered as schooners, ketch in its modern definition better describes the rig. The origin of the name is uncertain, but it could be from a custom of decorating the hawseholes in the form of large eyes; or, from the Scottish word *buckey*, oyster, which bugeyes were used to fish for. B-7, C-1b, DE-4, WAB

Bulbous Bow Just as the name implies. considered to be a recent development in ship design and seen on most modern ships, it is not all that new. The Navy takes credit for the first one on a (then) big ship, the U.S.S. *Delaware*, a battleship built in 1907. L-7

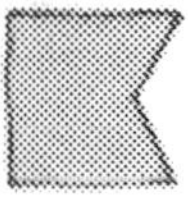

Bulkhead A shipboard wall or partition. (XV) Seen up into the XVII as two words, it comes from the Old Norse *balker*, partition. S-1, WO-1

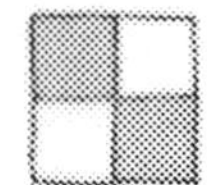

Bullnose A large closed chock on the stemhead. (1. XIX) Most likely a nickname, and as usual an apt one. It is usually well rounded or bolstered, and looks like a bull's nostril. N-4

Bullrope (1) On a square-rigger, a line for sending up or striking an upper mast. (XVII) (See *Toprope*) (2) Old but still current, (a) a line from the bowsprit to a mooring buoy, and (b) a line for a small boat to ride when secured to a boatboom. (XVIII p.e.) Why ''bull'' is not known, but possibly it implies strength. DE-5, WAB, JR

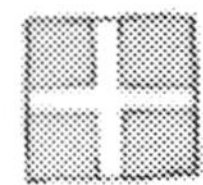

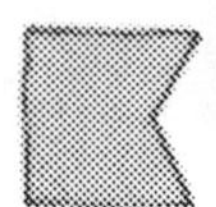

Bull's Eye A specially shaped grommet of wood or metal serving as a fairlead. (e. XVII p.e.) The origin is obscure; it probably was a nickname. (See ***Deadlight***) S-2

Bulwark A solid rail, usually consisting of extensions of the vessel's frames above deck-level and planked over. (XV) The word comes from Middle English ***bulwerke***, earlier roots being uncertain but of Nordic influence. S-1, WO-1

Bum Boat A small harbor craft used for peddling to, or ferrying, ships' crews, still extant in some ports. The term applied originally to boats so used on the Thames River, at and below London in the XVII century, and probably came from the Dutch word, ***bom***, bluff. WO-1

Bumkin (also ***Boomkin***) (1) Earlier, any of several short sparlike projections outboard of the hull, for various lines. (2) Modern meanings are (a) for yachts, a similar projection dead aft, usually for the mizzen sheet of a yawl or ketch (now becoming rarer), and (b) for research vessels, outboard projections for handling various equipment. (XVII) The word no doubt came direct from Flemish ***boomkin***, of the same meaning as the earlier use. A-2, WS-1

Bunk A built-in bed. (Possibly XVIII) The origin is obscure, but a likely possibility is that it came from the Dutch word ***bank***, meaning bench. WO-1, WS-1

Bunker (1) A compartment for fuel; earlier coal, now oil. (2) In vessels that carried coal as cargo, their fuel coal was called bunker, or bunkers. the same now applies for oil. (m. XIX) The origin is not known, but it could be Norwegian or Danish, the same word ***banke***, meaning hold. WO-1

Bunt The body of a sail, especially a square sail. The term is also a verb, said of a sail when bunched up for furling. (e. XVII p.e.) Its origin is the Old English word *byndel*, meaning bundle. S-2, DE-3

Bunting Loosely woven wool or cotton cloth from which flags were made, and sometimes still are. (e. XVII p.e.) The term comes from the Middle English *bonten*, to sift, leaving us to guess that this was an early use of this fabric. M-2, WS-2

Buntlines Lines on a square-rigger, attached to the foot of a sail, leading up its forward side, for furling. (e. XVII p.e.) The origin is the same as for bunt. S-2, WAB

Buoy A moored floating device, mainly to mark a channel, an obstruction, or hazard; also for mooring. (XVI p.e.) Earlier it was often spelled boy. The source is not certain, but a good guess is that it was the French word *boie*, chain or fetter. It is interesting to note that the word for buoy in most European languages is recognizable from Old French—and this includes the Russian word *buy*. (Small wonder when one thinks of their importance to mariners!) WO-1, WS-1

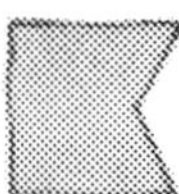

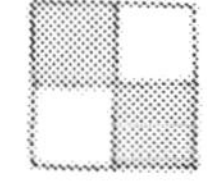

Burgee Now a term for the flag or pennant of a yacht or boat club, its earlier meaning, still sometimes applying in Britain, I am told, was the owner's, or house flag. In its present meaning the term dates from sometime in the XVIII century. (The oldest yacht club is the Royal Cork, dating from 1720, and it is probable that theirs is the oldest club burgee.) The term probably comes from the French *bourgeois*, which had an earlier meaning of master, or owner. WO-1

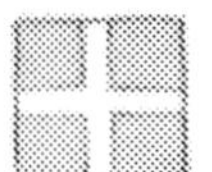

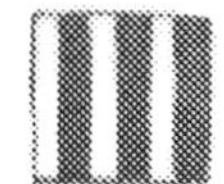

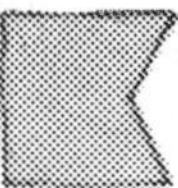

Burgoo has various definitions, possibly because it was different in different ships. (XVIII p.e.) One is oatmeal porridge, another hard tack and molasses, and a third, stew. One thing that seems certain is that it was not fancy. Its origin appears to be an Arabic word, ***burghul***, a dish of wheat, dried and boiled. WO-1, WW-1

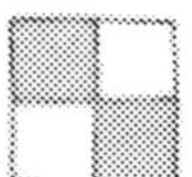

Burthen An old term to express a vessel's carrying capacity. (XII) At some time in the XVIth the word became burden. It came from the Old English ***byrpen***, meaning load. (See *Ton, Tun*) DE-3

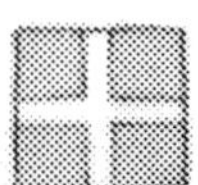

Burton A type of tackle purchase. (XV) It is believed to be a corruption of ***Breton***, but the connection is obscure. WO-1

Bury The part of the mast below the deck, or the inboard portion of the bowsprit. (e. XVII p.e.) The word comes from the Old English ***beorgan***, shelter or cover. WO-1

Bustle (1) A special kind of fairwater aft, on larger (and faster) merchant ships and some steam yachts, in the early XX century. (2) Another name for "blisters" built onto the sides of some merchant steamers to improve stability. (1. XIX) (3) A faired bulge on the bottom near the stern on some racing sailboats (XX).

The origin for all these, on good authority, is the lady's bustle of the late XIX. DVR

Butt A cask, often open-headed, for wine, grog, or water. (XIII) The word has several derivations, all of which appear to be related in application as well as in word origin: Late Latin ***buttis***, Anglo-French ***but***; Old French ***bot***; and, going back further, Greek ***butine***, all meaning the same thing. WS-1, DE-3

Buttock The rounded part of a ship's stern, an old term. (e. XVII p.e.) It came from the Middle English *buttok*. Whether this word applied to ships or to anatomy is uncertain—it could be both. S-2, DE-5

Buttocks are components in the design of any hull, lines of vertical planes passing through the hull. (e. XIX p.e.) The term appears to have come from buttock lines, the lines of a craft's afterbody. DE-5, WAB

Buy Ballot's Law A rule-of-thumb for determining variants of atmospheric pressure of a storm condition and of the location or direction of a storm center. (XIX) It is named for a Dutch scientist. B-6, D-4

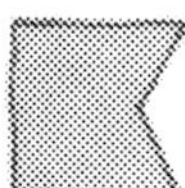

By This appears in many sailors' phrases, such as "by the wind," "by and large," etc., and was in use in Middle English, no doubt before. One scholar writes that the word itself came all the way from Sanskrit—*abbi*, meaning toward or to. WO-1, DE-5

By and Large Now not often heard in reference to ships, this was the term for sailing fairly close to the wind, "at speed" and with all sails well filled. (XVII p.e.) K-1, DE-3

By the Deep Language of the leadsman, reporting the depth when reading between the markers on his leadline. (XVIII p.e.) It is possibly a corruption of "by the dip." (See *Leadline*) F-1a, K-2

By the Wind An old term, still sometimes heard, for sailing close-hauled (XVI) DE-3

C.Q.R. Anchor Also known as a plow anchor (or plough in Britain), used extensively by yachts and many other small craft. It was invented in Great Britain, ca. 1930. The name given it is a non-presumptuous acronym for "secure." K-1

Cabin has many meanings; generally enclosed quarters. (XV p.e.) In British passenger ships it is the equivalent of our stateroom; in a U.S.N. or U.S.C.G. and most merchant ships it is the captain's quarters. In old sailing ships it was the officers' quarters. Earlier (c. XV-XVI) it meant a box-hammock suspended from the overhead, considered a luxury. S-2, SW-1, WAB

Cabin Sole (See *Sole*)

Cable (1) The anchor line, now chain or rope (or both, depending on the size of the craft), earlier of course always rope, and cable-laid. (XIII) The term came, via French, from the Latin word *capalum*, for halter. (2) A measure of distance: 720 feet or 120 fathoms, the standard length of an anchor cable for many years. (e. XVII p.e.) The origin in this sense is very probably related to the first use, above. Now rarely used, the term has been modified to mean about 100 fathoms, about one-tenth of a nautical mile. (See *Fathom*) (3) The name given to the heavy wire system used especially underwater, for long-distance telecommunications. This is made up of many individual wires, in layers, ergo in a sense cable-laid. M-1, WO-1, DE-3

Cable Laid In rope days on big ships, heavy lines, such as shrouds and hawsers, were usually made of three three-strand ropes, the cable being of opposite lay, or twist, to the components. (XVII p.e.) B-6, DE-3

Caboose Earlier, and mostly British, the galley deckhouse. (e. XVIII) It came from the Dutch ***kaban huis***, cabin house. This later bacame ***kabuys***, thence to Britain and "the Colonies."

For railroad buffs, the term first appeared in the U.S. as the name of the trainman's car in 1862. It is not used in this sense in Britain. WM-3, WO-1

Cabotage Coastwise trade, coastal navigation, or pilotage. (XV) The term has special significance, relating to various countries' laws relating to domestic coastwise trade. It comes from French and Spanish; the former, *caboter*, coast-sailing. DE-3

Cadet A student officer, in our Coast Guard and Merchant Marine, also in many navies. (XVIII) The word comes to us from French, thence from Latin, *capitulus*, a diminutive of *caput*, head, or chief. WO-1

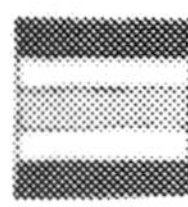

Cairn A type of shore beacon, earlier (and still) of rocks or stones, now of any material, in a pyramidal shape. (XIV p.e.) The term probably dates from Viking days. In English, it comes from the Celtic word *carn*, a pile of stone. WS-1

Calashee Watch An old term for "all hands on standby." One sailor's definition was an order to sleep on deck. (XVIII) It has several spellings and probably comes from Hindi. K-1, M-1

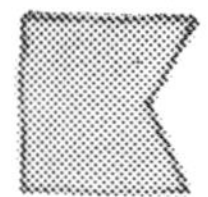

Camber The 'thwartships curving, or crowning, of the deck structure of a vessel. (XVII p.e.) Its origin is Latin, *camur*, curved, and it comes to us via Middle French, *cambre*, bent. S-2, DE-4

Camel (1) A type of floating dock used to lift a ship over shallows on entering or leaving port. The device was first used in Amsterdam, possibly as early as the XIV century. The origin of the term is believed to be from the name of an early dock, Camel. (2) A floating fender, of a log or a cluster of logs or beams, between a ship and her pier or quay when moored to the shore. (XVII p.e.) In France they were called *chameau*, camel, the reason for which is uncertain. D-3, DE-3

Canal A dredged or constructed water course. (XVII p.e.) This word comes intact from Old French, its meaning then being to convey liquid. It appears to be traceable to the Greek *kanne*, loosely translated as ditch or course. WO-1, WS-1

Can Buoy A cylindrical buoy. (e. XVII p.e.) The origin is a little vague, but an Anglo-Saxon and later a Middle English word for a drinking vessel or tankard was *canne*. In those days this type of container was usually straight-sided. S-2

Candy Stowage A XIXth century nickname for a special hold or locker for perishable or delicate cargo or stores. M-1, JR

Canoe A small, light, double-ended boat, thought of as originating in the Northeast and the eastern parts of the Middle West of North America. This is no doubt at least partially true, viz. the Indian birchbark canoe. The word is believed to come to us, however, from the West Indies: a Haitian word, *canoa*, meant boat. (XVI) WS-1, DE-4

Cant Generally, any member of a vessel's structure which is at an angle; used as a verb, adjective, or noun. (XIII) The word comes to us from Dutch, thence all the way back to Greek, *kanthos*, corner. M-2, DE-5

Cant Frame A vessel's frame that is not at right-angles with the keel, i.e., at the forward and after ends. (XIII) The derivation is the same as for cant. DE-3, DE-4

Canvas Cotton cloth from which sails were made, also awnings, covers, dodgers, hammocks, etc. It is an interesting term. First, to trace it back, it came from Middle English *canevas*, but then the word meant hemp, and goes back to the Greek *kaphasis*, and possibly to Sanskrit *cana*, both meaning hemp. It is not clear when it was used to define sail cloth (probably XVII p.e.). DE-3, WS-1

Now, coming back to 1851, one of the reasons for the renowned success of the schooner *America* in her famous race in the Solent was that she had cotton canvas sails, which were flatter and less porous, hence more efficient than those of her British competitors, whose "canvas" was of hemp. R-2

Capsize hardly needs definition. (XIII) An earlier spelling was capasize, and it probably came from the Spanish word *capuzan*, to sink. (The Nova Scotian word, present and past tense, is "upsot.") WO-1, JR

Capstan The large vertical-axis drum-head "engine" by which anchors were hoisted, and some sails and their yards, cargo, and heavy equipment were handled. (e. XVII p.e.) Earlier there appeared to be several spellings, a common one being capastan. The origin appears to be Portuguese, *cabestan*, it being traceable to the Latin word *capistrare*, to fasten with rope. S-2, WS-1

Captain The comanding officer of any vessel, also an officer's rank in the Navy and Coast Guard. (Possibly XI, certainly XVII) It came to us via Old French *chevetagne*, chieftan, from the Latin *caput*, head or leading officer. S-1, WO-1

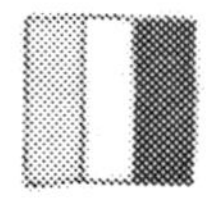

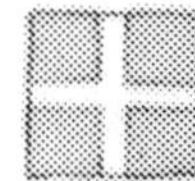

Caravel A small merchant vessel, seen mostly in the Mediterranean, but also sailed offshore by the Spanish and Portuguese. (XIV-XVII) The term appears to come from the Spanish *carrabala*, a type of ship, thence back to the Greek *karabos*, a light ship. WS-1

Cardinal Points The four principal points of the compass. This term is difficult to trace, but its use probably goes back to the XVI century (p.e.), then relating to the four winds. Its current meaning is from the XVIII. The word comes from the Latin *cardinalis*, principal. WO-1, DE-3

Careen To tip a vessel to a steep angle, to repair or work on her bottom. (e. XVII p.e.) It comes from the French word *carene*, of the same meaning, and can be loosely traced back, through Latin and Greek, to Sanskrit. S-2, WO-1

Cargo is the general term for lading, or freight, carried by a merchant ship. (XVII p.e.) The origin is Latin, *carricum*, load. It may have come into English via Gascon French. One word scholar asks why cargo pertains to ships, and shipments to land conveyances. WO-1

Carlings Fore-and-aft timbers between the deck beams, earlier often seen as carlins, and carlines. (1. XIV) The origin is uncertain; it appears to be Icelandic. S-1, S-2

Carpenter A warrant officer classification in the Sea Services and a petty officer's rating in merchant ships. His responsibilities were, and are, many: mainly the maintenance of all the ship's deck gear, including her boats and fixed rigging. The term has been in use in maritime circles from the XVI century; the general word goes back to the Latin *carpenterius*, meaning carriage maker. WO-1, N-4

Carrack A type of merchant ship, often armed, of the XIV to XVII centuries. The word comes from the Old French *caraque*, of the same meaning, and could go back to Arabic. WO-1

Carrick Bend Now an ornamental knot, it was once a method of bending a line to a heavier one. (XVII p.e.) The term's origin is obscure, but it could be related to *carrack*. DE-3

Carronade A special, short, light, ship's cannon. It got its name from the Carron Iron Works, in Carron, Scotland, where it was first made in 1779. WS-1

Carry On Now an order, used mostly in the Navy, to continue with work. Earlier it meant to keep the sails on, to "keep her moving." (XVIII p.e.) N-4

Carvel (1) A type of wooden ship and boat construction, in which the planking is flush and smooth. The origin of the term is vague at best, but it could be about the XII century and come from the Old Norse word for this technique, *karfi*. WO-1, DE-5 (2) Another earlier name for *Caravel*. The term also could have come from Portuguese, as the caravel (also carvel), a Portuguese vessel-type, was so constructed. WAB

Cast (1) An old term rarely heard today, for turning a vessel. It came, via Middle English, from Old Norse, *kasta*, warp. (2) To throw, as a line (never, in spite of the poets, the anchor). In this sense the origin is Middle English, *casten*, to throw. WS-1, WW-1

Cat (1) To hoist an anchor to its cathead; also a short name for the cathead. (XVIII p.e.) M-2 (2) A name given to the rig of a catboat. (3) The short name for the dreaded cat-o'-nine-tails.

Catamaran Any two-hulled craft. The origin of the concept is not known, but it certainly goes back many centuries. The word is believed to come from Tamil (East Indian), *kattamaram*. WM-1

Catboat A sailboat of our East Coast, a craft of many uses; shallow draft, very beamy, with centerboard and rigged with a large mainsail and no jib. They were in wide use from Chesapeake Bay northward (or east) from about 1850 until after 1900, but are still not uncommon. No one seems sure of the origin of the name, but one expert guesses they were named after a Dutch craft, *katboot*, of which the mast was "in the eyes," i.e., well forward. The term applies both to the boat and its rig. JG

Cat Davit A small davit in the bow, which post-dates the cathead, used mainly to assist in housing an anchor. (m. XIX) The origin of the term seems clear. N-4

Catharpins Lines laced around the shrouds near the masthead of a sailing ship, to reduce slack. (e. XVII p.e.) Earlier there were several spellings, most often catharpings. The origin of the term is not known. M-2, S-2

Catheads Stout beams projecting on both bows of sailing ships, used in hoisting and housing the anchors. (c. XVI) They got their name from the custom, of unknown origin, of decorating them with carved or cast lions' heads, believed to be for good luck. WO-1, DE-4

Catholes *(also Cat Holes)* Closed chocks or hawse holes on the quarters of older sailing ships, for heavy lines. (XVIII p.e.) The term appears to have been a nick-name, and may have reference to quarter galleries. D-4, K-1

Cat-o'-Nine-Tails The terrible whip with which sailors were flogged. It is believed that its origin was in Egypt, where the cat was sacred, and even then was believed to have nine lives. The Egyptians were said to believe that by scourging with cat hide, good passed from the whip to the victim. A possible derivation is Late Latin, *catonus*, a scourge loaded with lead. Its dreaded nickname was "cat." K-1, L-8

Cat Rig The rig of a catboat, ergo any similar fore-and-aft rig with a mast with a minimum of standing rigging, and no headsails. (See *Catboat*)

Catwalk A walkway above deck-level, running fore-and-aft, to enable the crew to avoid "no-man's-land" in rough weather. Seen first aboard the big square-riggers of the late XIX, these later became common on tankers. The origin of the term is unknown, but it does imply the nimbleness of a cat. It was also known as a monkey bridge. DE-3, DE-5

Caulk To make seams watertight by driving in any of various appropriate materials. (XV) An earlier spelling was calk. It probably had its origin in Latin, *calcare*, to force down with pressure, and came into English from Old French. S-2, WO-1

Caulk-Off is a slang term for taking a nap. (XVII p.e.) Nowadays sometimes misspelled and mispronounced "cork-off," it undoubtedly got its start from the fact that if a sailor laid down on deck for any length of time, the caulking would leave a stain on his clothing. JR

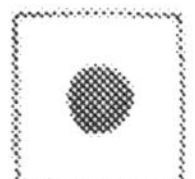

Cavil (See *Kevel*) WW-1

Ceiling The interior planking or plating affixed to a ship's frames. (XV) This term came from the Middle English *celen*, meaning screen or lining. S-1, DE-4

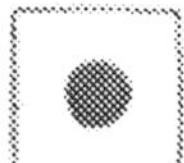

Centerboard A sailboat keel that can be raised or lowered; either the only keel or a supplement to a fixed keel. As we know it, it was invented and first used in Boston waters, ca. 1774 C-1b, K-1, WAB

Chafe The enemy of all mariners, especially those "in sail," it is damage caused by friction. (e. XVII p.e.) The term comes from Middle English, *chaufe*, thence from Old French, *chaufer*, to make warm by rubbing, and goes back to Latin, *calefacare*, to warm. S-2, WO-1

Chains, The The leadsman's station over the side, so named because this was on a channel, or chain-wale. (e. XVII p.e.) (See *Channel*) S-2, WO-1

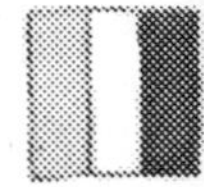

Chandler The shoreside purveyor to all the needs of a ship in port. The term was seen in the XIV century, when a chandler was a maker and seller of candles, then virtually the only source of illumination. From that period, his services were expanded to include all supplies. The word is Middle English and Old Modern English for candle-maker, and came from the Old French *chandelier*, of this same meaning. WO-1

Channel (1) A watercourse, natural or dredged. In its present sense the word was in use in the XVI century, although variations on the meaning were seen in the XIII. It comes from Old French, *chanel*, watercourse. (2) Part of the hull of a sailing ship. A corruption or contraction of the term chain-wale, an extra-thick or built-up plank essential to the securing of the shrouds. (p. XII) WO-1

Channel Fever is and was like spring fever, although probably more sanguine. Now a general term, it was the word for the euphoria felt by English seamen upon entering the English Channel from sea, on the last stretch for home. V-1b, KK

Chantey (also ***Chanty, Shanty***) A shipboard song, sung while at a specific job, such as walking a capstan, hoisting sail, etc. A "chanteyman" would usually lead the singing, and the crew or work-party would join in. The custom was known in the XVI century; the word came from the French *chanter*, to sing. WO-1

Chapelling (*also Chappelling*) Involuntary tacking or going aback, in a square-rigger, due to poor steering or a sudden shift of wind. (XVIII p.e.) The term comes from the French *faire chapelle*, the meaning of which is believed to be the same, but the translation is unclear. WO-1

Chapels Grooves in a built-up mast. (XVIII p.e.) The derivation of this term is uncertain; it may be from the word *chapelet*, Middle English, Old English, and Old French, one meaning in all these being support. P-1b, DE-3

Charley Noble is the nickname for the galley smokepipe. Various guesses have been made on this, everyone agreeing that somebody in the early XIX century took great pride in keeping the brass or copper (or possibly both) galley-stack brightly shined. You have some choices here: he was "identified" variously as a cook, an officer or mate, or a captain, British or American, of a naval or merchant vessel. L-8, WO-1

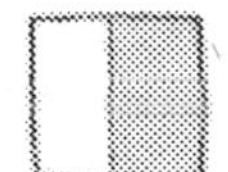

Chart The mariner's map. (XIV) This term comes from the French *charte*, map; and can be traced to Greek, *khartes*, map. The term could be of Egyptian origin. WO-1

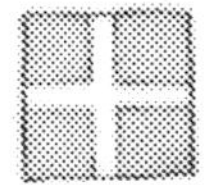

Charter To lease or rent, or the leasing or renting of, a ship or boat. (XIII) The term comes, via Old French, *chartie*, from the Latin *chartula*, a diminutive of *charta*, document. WO-1

Charter Party The master document of a charter agreement. (XV) This term comes from the French *charte partie*, divided document, and obviously is related to charter. DE-3

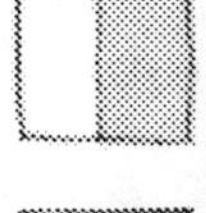

Cheeks (1) Supports for the trestletrees on a sailing ship's masts. (XIV) (2) The sides of a block. (XVII p.e.) (See *Block*) The origin, in the nautical sense, for both, is uncertain. The word came from Old English, *ceace*, cheek, and could have these meanings. A-2, M-2

Chernikief Log An impellor-type underwater device, usually retractable, to measure speed and distance run. It was invented by an officer of the Russian Imperial Navy, and developed by the British Navy, ca. 1917. NMMG

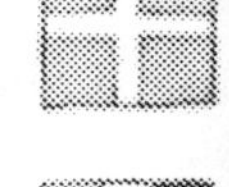

Chess Trees (also *Chesstrees*) Short projections from the topsides of a square-rigger, with blocks or built-in sheaves on their ends, for the leads of the braces. (XVII) The term appears to be related to the French *chassis*, frame. S-1, DE-3

Chine Broadly, the intersection of the topside and the bottom. (XIV) Also the term for longitudinal rib-like strips on the bottoms of various types of modern high-speed motorboats. The origin is Old French, *eschine*, spine or backbone. WO-1

Chinse A variation of *chink*, temporary caulking. (e. XVII p.e.) The word is possibly a corruption of an early English dialect word, *chinch*, of the same sense. (See *Devil*) M-2, DE-5

Chip Log The name for the device used in earlier days, for measuring distance travelled. A block of wood, or chip, fastened to a line by a bridle, was allowed to run out over the stern; the amount of line run was measured in time with a sand-glass. The line was knotted at specific intervals. (See *Knot*) K-1, T-1

Chips The nickname for the ship's carpenter. (Probably e. XVIII) B-6, K-1

Chit A "marker," or invoice for goods and services aboard ship. (XVIII) The word probably came into English on the British ships sailing to and from India. Its origin may have been Sanskrit; it came direct from the Hindi word *chitthi*, letter or note. WO-1

Chock (1) A type of fairlead. (XIV) (2) To wedge any moveable object in order to hold it steady. (Possibly XVI) In both senses, the word is believed to have come from the Old French *coche*, block of wood. S-1, WO-1

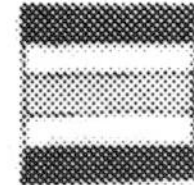

Chock-a-Block An old term, still used, for any sail, flag, or gear hoisted fully. (e. XVII p.e.) DE-3

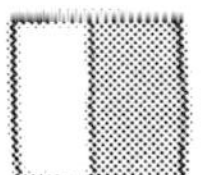

Choking the Luff Putting the fall line of a tackle inside the "parts," as a fast release stopper. (XVIII p.e.) The term very possibly refers to the choke of a block and to a luff tackle. (See *Block*) F-1b

Chow A sailor's word for food or a meal. (XIX, p.e.) It may well be a corruption of the South China pidgin word *chow-chow*, food, from clipper-ship days or earlier. WM-3

Chronometer A highly accurate clock used in navigation, which also served as a ship's master clock. While in use on shipboard and ashore some time earlier, it was not highly enough developed to be considered dependable until the mid-XIX century. The word is made-up from the Greek *chronos*, time, and *metron*, measure. WS-1

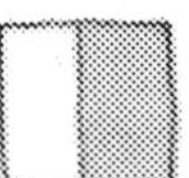

Clamp A fore-and-aft structural member of a vessel's framing, inboard of the frames and supporting the deck beams. (XV) The origin may have been Dutch, *klamp*, fastening, or Anglo-Saxon, *clam*, bond, or possibly both. S-1, DE-4

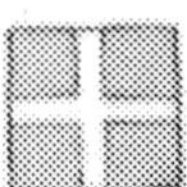

Clap On To add on, i.e., more sail, more hands on a line, a better purchase. (XIX p.e.) The words appear to come from the Old Norse *klappan*, to act quickly. WS-1, DE-3

Cleading Casing for buoyancy tanks for a lifeboat. (m. XIX p.e.) The word is an old one, coming from Scottish, thence from Old Norse. D-4, K-1

Clean Bill of Health A document indicating that a vessel has no serious illness on board and is in a generally healthy condition. (XVIII) F-1b

Cleat A horn-shaped piece of wood or metal, to which a line may be made fast. (XVI p.e.) It comes from Old English, the same word with a similar meaning. WO-1

Clew Lower or leeward corner of a sail. (e. XVII p.e.) The word is derived from Old English and Old Norse, the latter word being *kle*, of this same meaning. S-2, WO-1

Clinker (also *Clinker-Built*) A method of ship and boat construction dating from Viking-ship days, of overlapping planks or strakes. (XVI) A British term is clench-built, and the word relationship is apparent, as both are derived from Old English, *klenken*, to hold fast. (See *Lapstrake*) WS-1

Clinometer A device for measuring the angle of roll, heel, or list. (XIX) The term is made-up, from the Greek *clino*, cause to lean, and *metron*, measure. DE-4

Clipper (also Clipper Ship) The famed and fast square-rigged ships, of very fine lines, of the mid-to-late XIX century. The term was used before this time, i.e., the Baltimore clipper. A romantic supposition is that the term came from a corruption of the name of a well-known French ship named the *Cleopatra cum Antonio*, which was very fast and handsome. Her name was said to have been shortened by those who knew her, to *clipster*, and then to *clipper*. WO-1

Clothing An old term for the rigging holding the bowsprit in place. (XVIII p.e.) M-4, S-3

Club Any of several short spars on sailing craft, seen in various functions from the XVIII century to the present. A good guess is that the word came from the Middle English *clubbe*, cudgel or short staff. DE-4

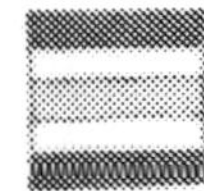

Clubbing An old term for dredging an anchor, itself an earlier technique of purposely dragging an anchor over the bottom to reduce speed. (e. XIX p.e.) The origin is not known. S-2, DE-3

Clump Block A heavy and rounded single-sheave block with wide sheave, especially for use with headsail sheets of large sailing vessels. (XIX p.e.) The word appears to have come from Old English, *clympre*, lumpy. DE-4, S-3

Coaming The ridge surrounding a hatch, companionway, or, more recently, a cockpit. (e. XVII p.e.) Earlier it had other spellings, such as combing and coming; the latter coming as is from Middle English, possibly with the same meaning. It could have originated in Old High German. S-2, DE-4

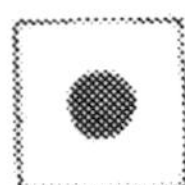

Cockbill (1) or more properly a-cockbill, is the term for sloping the yards of a square rigger. This was done for two reasons, one as a gesture of mourning, and the other, more practical, to avoid fouling the spars of another vessel tied-up alongside. B-1 (2) Also a term for hanging the anchor from the cathead (XVII p.e.). DE-3

Cockboat Any small ship's-boat of past years, and I am told still heard in Britain. (XV) It can be traced, via Old French and Latin, to the Greek *koykn*, a type of small boat. WS-1, DE-3

Cockpit Now any small welldeck especially on small craft. Formerly it was a compartment on a warship where the wounded and ill were tended. It probably was nicknamed for the arena where fighting cocks did their bit, the connection for which is obscure. WO-1

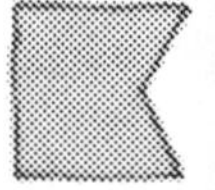

Coffee Grinder A large deck winch on a modern racing yacht, on which the cranks are on a vertical standard, and could be said to resemble those of an old-fashioned coffee mill. (m. XX) R-3

Coil To wind rope, or to lay it out, in a series of rings; also the result of so doing. (e. XVII p.e.) The word came from Old French, *coilir*, to gather. M-2, WO-1

Coir Cordage made of coconut fiber, which floats (for a time), is light, and has great stretch. (XIII) It is not known when coir was first used, but it appears to be a long time ago. The word comes from Malay, *kayen*, rope. DE-4

Collar An eye of a stay or shroud that goes over the masthead; also a ring on the mast to which stays are secured. The word goes back, via Middle English and Old French, to the Latin *collare*, but its origin in the nautical sense is not known. M-2, DE-3

Collision at Sea Can Ruin Your Entire Day

This simple statement, according to one naval historian, is attributed to Thucydides, a Greek seaman, adventurer, and statesman of the IV century B.C. H-4

Colors

(1) The ensign. When the term came into use in this sense is uncertain, but flags, banners, and other devices have been used for identification and decoration from at least Roman days. (2) The ceremony or simple act of hoisting and lowering the ensign in the morning and evening. The customary times of 0800 and sunset were established by the Navy in the 1880s. A similar routine is followed in the ship world and by yacht people, as is practicable. The term is derived from the Latin *colorem*, interestingly a word for command. L-8, WO-1

Come About

To change course by tacking, in a sailing craft. This term appeared in the XVI century, but in a different sense; it then meant a shift of the wind. As to tacking, it very probably changed to this meaning with the advent of the fore-and-aft rig. DE-3

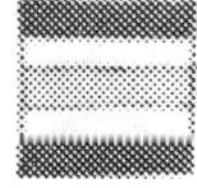

Commander

(1) An officer's rank in the Navy and Coast Guard (the lowest ranking "brass hat"). (XIX) N-4 (2) A title sometimes used in the British merchant service for the captain, particularly of larger ships in which several officers had master's papers. (3) A large, heavy mallet; a tool believed to have originated with shipbuilding. (XVIII p.e.) DE-3 The derivation, via Old French, is Latin, *commandare*, command. One translation of the Old French word is to make move, which appears to apply in all senses. (See *Beetle*) DE-3

Commission, In

Said of a Sea Services vessel in full active service, the term is also loosely used colloquially for merchant and commercial ships, and yachts. This designation of a vessel's status goes back at least to the early XVIII century for the British Navy, and applied to our ships as our infant navy came into being. N-4

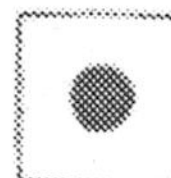

Commodore A special rank in the Navy, senior to the rank of captain. Navy people also use the term unofficially for the senior captain in a group of ships, regardless of his actual rank. In the Merchant Marine it is usually the title given to the company's senior captain. In yachting circles this is the title of the "president" of a yacht club. (XVII) The origin of the word is uncertain; it could be Dutch, ***komandem*** commander. WO-1

Companionway A ladderway through a hatch, to the next deck below or above. An earlier definition for companion was a hatch or skylight, also for a covering over a hatch. The term may have come from the Dutch ***kamagne***, for quarterdeck or poopdeck; or possibly from French and Italian for pantry or storeroom: *compagne* and *compagna*. WO-1

Compass The vital instrument that points the way, be it the simplest magnetic or a sophisticated gyroscope. (XIV) There are several versions of the word's origin, involving the Nordic and Romance languages. One commonly agreed on is the Late Latin *compassare*, circle. M-2, WO-1

Con To direct the movements of a vessel underway. (e. XVII p.e.) The officer so doing is said to be "at the con" or to "have the con," Earlier spellings were conn and cond. The word comes from the Old French *conduire*, to conduct, and has two earlier roots: Anglo-Saxon, *connan*, control; and Latin, *conducere*, to conduct. S-2, WO-1

Console The control center on the bridge of a modern power craft, where all the devices and instruments are in easy reach of one man. The word came into sailors' language, as did the concept, very recently, and it would seem apparent that it was named after the organ console. WO-1

Contlines The spiral grooves between the strands of laid cordage. (XVIII p.e.) It is a corruption of the earlier term cant line, so named because they are at an angle. (See *Cant*) B-1, DE-3

Convoy To accompany or escort, or a group of ships steaming together, usually under protection. (XVI) Its origin, via Middle English, is the French *convoyer*, to convoy or conduct. WO-1, WS-1

Cooper A crew member in earlier days who made and mantained the barrels for ship's stores, cargo, and powder. (XIV) He was an especially important man in a whaler's crew, as he made the barrels for the whale oil. The term came from Middle Dutch, *kuper*, also from German, and goes back to the Latin *cuparius*, barrel maker. S-2, WO-1

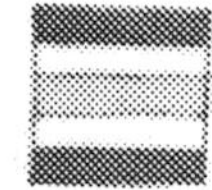

Cordage A general term for all rope and small stuff. (XIII) This term goes back to Greek, *khorde*, cord, and came into English from Old French, *corde*. M-2, WO-1

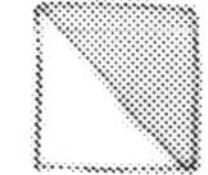

Corinthian Now simply an amateur sailor and rarely referred to as such; commonly heard when there were many professionals in the yacht world. (Probably XIX) The word was seen in Middle English, but goes back in significance to the athletes of Corinth. DE-4

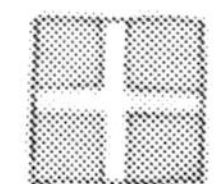

Corposant A ball or streak of light sometimes seen aloft at sea, caused by static electricity under some atmospheric conditions. (XVII) The word comes, via Italian, Portuguese, and Spanish, from Latin, *corpo sanctus*, holy body. (See *Saint Elmo's Fire*) DE-4, WO-1

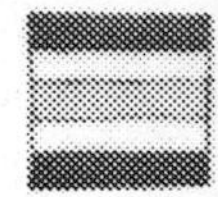

Corsair An especially independent privateer, usually in the Mediterranean Sea. (XIV) The word comes from the French *corsaire*, raid. WS-1

Corvette In sailing-ship days, a ship-rigged "one-decker," smaller, and supposedly faster than a frigate. (XVII) In present times it is a patrol and escort ship, usually smaller and more lightly armed than a destroyer. The word came directly from the French, of the same early meaning, and can be traced to Early Dutch, and, remotely, to Latin. WO-1, WS-1

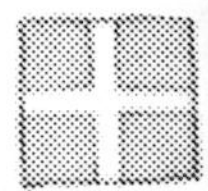

Counter The definitions of this term vary, but a safe one is the underside of the after overhang, including the transom if any. A reason for the difficulty in defining is the changing of ships' and boats' sterns since the XVI and XVII centuries, when the term appeared. The origin is uncertain too, but it may be a simple one: the French term *contre arcasse*, the curves of the stern. S-2, WO-1, WW-1

Course (1) Direction. (XIII) It came from Old French, the same word and meaning, and thence from the Latin *cursus*, direction. (2) The courses are the lowest square sails on all masts of a square-rigger. (XV) The origin in this sense is uncertain, but it may be Old French, *cours*, cause to run. S-1, W-2, WO-1

Covering Board The deck plank over the frame-heads of any wooden craft, therefore the outermost deck plank. (XVIII p.e.) Its definition seems to identify its origin. S-3

Cove Stripe A painted or guilded ornamental band on the hull, usually close to the sheer line. It was and is sometimes a groove. (probably XVIII) It may have been named for a tool used for cutting a groove, called a coving plane. D-3, S-3

Cowl The bell-shaped top of a ship's or boat's ventilator. (XIX) The word came, via Old English and Old French, from the Latin *cucillus*, hood. WO-1

Coxwain Over the years this has been the title of a leading seaman or petty officer in charge of a ship's boat. (Possibly XIII) It was for many years the name of the Navy and Coast Guard rating for boatswain's mate third class. The term is a composite, from Middle English *coq*, ship's boat, and *swain*, attendant. S-2, WO-1

It now, also, is the title of the helmsman of a racing shell.

Cradle The structure by which vessels were, and smaller craft are, held upright and steady when out of the water, as in drydock or "up on the ways." (e. XVII p.e.) The term came from the Anglo-Saxon *cradl*, or *cradel*, meaning basket, but which also is believed to have meant a ship's (also a baby's) cradle. S-2, WS-1

Craft is a very general word. In the nautical sense it refers to virtually all ships and boats, large or small. (XVII p.e.) It comes from Old English, *craeft*, which is believed to refer not only to boats and ships but to the skills required to build them. M-2, DE-3

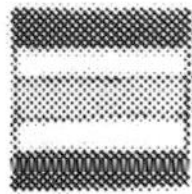

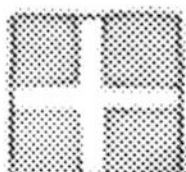

Crane A lifting device, for cargo and heavy gear. Rarely seen on ocean-going vessels before the XIX century, as sailing ships used various tackles from their yards or got shoreside help, cranes have been in use in dockyards and shipyards for a long time. The word comes, via Middle English, from the Old English *cran*, of the same sense, and could go back to Greek. DE-4, DE-5

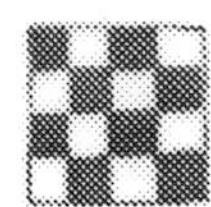

Cranky (also ***Crank***) An adjective for any craft of low or poor stability. (XVII) The word comes from Old English, *cringan*, one meaning of which was to become weak or delicate. WO-1

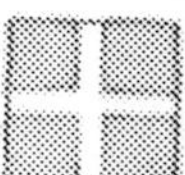

Cranse-Iron The fitting on a sailing vessel's bowsprit for the jibboom; also later one type of a hinge-fitting for a yard on its mast. (Probably XVII) This term appears to come from the Dutch word ***krans***, meaning garland. DE-3

Crew Broadly, a ship's people other than the captain and officers. (XVII) The word came, via Middle English and Old French, from the Latin *crescere*, to increase or grow. The significance of this is simply that most ships for several centuries had only skeleton crews as regulars, and "filled out" for voyages by various forms of recruitment (not always gentle). An earlier translation of crew was reenforcement. (See *Shanghai*) WO-1

Cringle A ropework loop on the edge of a sail, especially for reefing. (e. XVII p.e.) This word travelled a bit. Its origin was Old English, *cranc*, bent, then it went to German and Dutch, ***kringle***, ring, then back to English. S-2, WO-1

Cross Head (also *Crosshead*) The yoke-like device on the rudder-head of various types of small craft for steering with handlines. It probably came into being with the first stern rudders, in the XI century, but the term was not seen until much later. (See *Yoke*) DE-5

Crossjack The course sail on the aftermost mast of a square-rigged ship. (XIV) Known by several short spellings, the most phonetic and best known being *crojick*. The origin of the term is uncertain; however, it was sometimes called a cross-sail, and was relatively small. (See *Jack*) S-1

Crosstrees 'Thwartship timbers over the trestle-trees on the mast of a sailing ship. (XVII) The origin is vague: cross is undoubtedly a shortening of across, and tree was and is a word for many devices made of wood. S-2, WO-1

Crowfoot Earlier, a system of lines, gathered at one end and spread at the other, to support a sail or yard. (e. XVII p.e.) More modern, a technique for tabling a sail to strengthen stress points. In the earlier sense, the word came from Middle English, *crowfote*, of the same meaning. (See *Tabling*) A-2, M-2, DE-5

Crow's Nest The lookout station at the highest practicable point aloft. (XVIII p.e.) One guess for this term is that some Norse vessels carried ravens in cages; when in doubt as to the whereabouts of land, the skipper ordered the cages hoisted aloft and the birds released, and then followed their direction to shore. DE-3, Pub-3

Cruise A simple definition is to wander, whatever the reason. In the XVII century, when the word was first in use, it usually meant going to sea for warlike purposes, hence cruiser. The word came from the Dutch *kruizer*, to cross. S-2, WO-1

Crutch A support for a spar. The term appears to go back to Viking days. A root word was *krykkia*, Old Norse for a forked or crooked timber, and its original sense was said to be nautical. WO-1

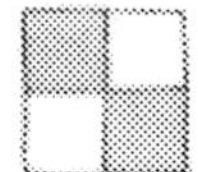

Cuddy Variously defined; a safe one is a small compartment or cabin. (XVII) It appears to come from Old French, *cabute*, and early Dutch, *kabute*, small cabin. WO-1

Cunningham An adjustment device or a cringle and lace-line above the tack of a fore-and-aft sail, to "fine-tune" its shape. It is a modern device, mostly for racing boats, and is named for its inventor Briggs Cunningham, a well-known sailor. (m. XX) R-3

Cut and Run originally meant to cut the anchor cable, or to cut the gaskets to make sail, to get under way in a hurry. (Probably XVII) L-4

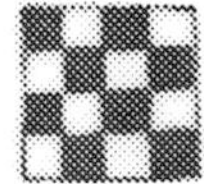

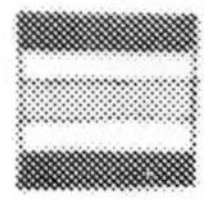

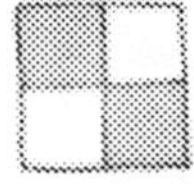

Cutlass The shortsword that was for many years the basic sidearm of the seagoing warrior or man-o'-war's-man. When the word was first used in English is not certain—it was possibly in the XVII century—but the source is clear: Old French, *coutelas*, and that came from the Latin *cultellus*, short sword. WO-1

Cutter (1) A fast, small ocean-going vessel, usually a government type (i.e., Coast Guard and earlier the Revenue Service) for patrolling and police duties. (XVIII) (2) A single-masted sailboat, fore-and-aft rigged, the mast of which is located farther aft than that of a sloop, and which usually is rigged for two or more headsails. (Mid XIX) (3) A ship's pulling boat, of eight oars or more, also rigged for sail; usually lug rigged. (XVIII p.e.) The term appears to come from the Middle English *kittere*, a sharp boat. K-1, WO-1

Cutwater As the term implies, the part of the stem at the water's edge and below. (e. XVII p.e.) M-2

Dacron Synthetic polyester fabric used for most modern sails, and for some types of cordage. (m. XX) It is a trade name, registered by DuPont. DE-5

Dan Buoy A temporary buoy for any of several purposes, usually associated with fishing, or sometimes anchoring. (XVIII p.e.) The origin of Dan in this connection is obscure; it is said to be Daniel, but whether biblical or otherwise does not seem to be recorded. S-3, WW-1

Dasher Block A small block at the aftermost gaff peak of a sailing vessel, used for the ensign, also for signal hoists. It is also a block for a studding sail boom outhaul. In both applications it was also called a jewel block, possibly because of its small size. The derivation of dasher is not known. (l. XVIII) B-4, JR

Davy Jones's Locker (also *Davy Jones. . .*) The bottom of the sea. Davy is the legendary evil spirit of the sea. He was conjured up in the XVII or XVIII century, but where his name came from is uncertain. A good guess is that West Indian sailors invented him, and that it could be a corruption of Devil Jonah, or possibly Duffy Jonah, duffy being a British West Indian word for devil. WO-1

Davits A pair of cranes for hoisting and lowering a ship's boats. The word was seen in the early XVII century, the spelling then having been David; which appears to bear out a contention that someone named David invented them. Who he was is not known. S-2, WS-1

Day's Work The navigator's working day, being from his noon sights and position to those of the following day. (XVIII p.e.) F-1b

Deadeye (also ***Dead Eye***, and earlier, ***Dead Man's Eye***) A rounded piece of hardwood with three holes in a triangular pattern, spliced into the lower ends of the shrouds and by which they were fastened to the chain plates with lanyards. (XVI) The origin is uncertain; it could be a nickname, due to the similarity to a man's face. Another guess is that it had no moving parts. (See ***Deadlight***) S-2, DE-3

Dead Horse was a name for the period of time after a ship's sailing that her crew was working off advanced wages, often a month or more. (XVIII p.e.) When it was ended, the custom in some British ships was to celebrate by making an effigy of a horse from scrap material, hoisting it aloft and outboard, lighting it afire, and cutting it adrift. S-3, DE-3

Deadlight (1) A fixed piece of glass in a door, the deck, etc., for added light. Also sometimes called a bullseye. (XVIII p.e.) One of the many meanings of the word dead, which is fairly common in the mariner's world, is immobile or inactive. DE-3 (2) Also a wooden, and later steel, cover for a portlight or porthole, to protect it from storm or battle damage and to "darken ship." (XIX) It is also called a storm port or a battleport. K-1, JR

Deadman The loose, often frayed, end of a line. Also an improperly caulked seam. (And also an empty bottle.) (XIX p.e.) S-3, DE-3

Dead Reckoning A procedure of navigation, using course, speed, and drift data or estimates. (e. XVII p.e.) The term is believed simply to be a corruption of deduced reckoning. WM-3

Deadrise The vertical distance from the point of intersection of the top of the keel to the turn of the bilge. (e. XVIII p.e.) The term's origin is not known. S-3

Deadwater The part of a vessel's stern wake directly and immediately aft of the vessel; in effect, negative turbulence. (XV) S-2, WO-1

Deadwood The after part of the hull underwater, where it is shaped into the rudder post (XVIII p.e.) DE-3

Deck What you walk on or what shelters you aboard ship. (XV) It formerly meant only a covering, or roof, not the modern sense of a platform. The term comes from the Middle Dutch word *dec*, meaning roof. S-1, WO-1

Deep Six To give an object the deep six is to throw it overboard. It is a slang term, the origin of which is not known. By the deep six is the leadsman's report of six fathoms depth. (XVIII) N-4, JR

Demurrage The name given to the delay of a vessel beyond the agreed terms for delivering cargo for loading or accepting unloaded cargo; also the term for the charges assessed. (XVII p.e.) The word comes from the French *demur*, delay. DE-3

Derelict An abandoned floating vessel. The word apparently came direct from Latin, *derelictus*, forsaken. When it came into English is uncertain. (Perhaps XVII) WS-1, WO-1

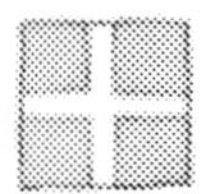

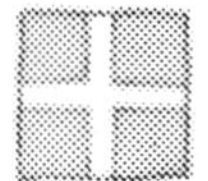

Derrick A lever system for handling cargo, stores, boats, etc. It is doubtful that the term was in use for marine applications until the XIX century, but the word goes back to the XVI, and is derived from the name of a well-known English hangman. WS-1

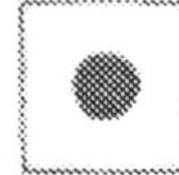

Destroyer A relatively light and always fast combat ship, called by some the workhorse of the navies. The earlier name, when the type was first developed by the U.S., British, and European navies, was torpedo boat destroyer, the mission of which was obvious. The first American destroyer was the U.S.S. *Farragut*, of 273 tons, built in 1898. N-4, L-6

Devil There seems to be no certainty of a definition of this term. However, all the guesses have two things in common: it was a seam, and a difficult one to work on. Of the several definitions I have encountered, here are three: (a) the outboard seam on deck, (b) the garboard seam, and (c) any seam below the channels which sometimes had to be caulked or otherwise worked on (chinsed) while a ship was underway. It would seem that one of the last two is the most likely, and the name apt. (Possibly XVII) M-1, WW-1

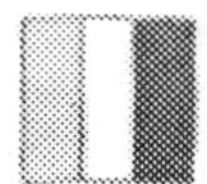

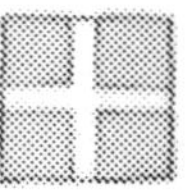

Diaper Plate A plate, bolted, not riveted or welded, in a place near the rudder post, for access for inspection and repair. An appropriate one, the term came into being with iron and steel ships. (XIX) DVR

Dido, Cutting a Now a shoresider for frivolously "acting up," this was a British phrase originating in their navy, honoring H.M.S. *Dido*, a very fast and nimble ship, whose captain enjoyed sailing circles around the fleet, ca. 1800. K-1

Diesel is hardly a nautical term, but this engine is almost a way of life for all sorts and sizes of craft. It was named for its inventor, Rudolph Diesel, and was first displayed in Munich in 1898. DE-1

Dinghy Any of several types of small boats, round-bottomed and usually light and nimble. (Possibly XVIII) The word comes from the Hindi *dinhi* or *dengi*, a diminutive for the name of a type of vessel. WO-1

Dioptric Light The beam of light from a buoy or lighthouse, which is concentrated by prisms or lenses. (XVIII) The word is adopted from the Greek *dioprikos*, roughly, refraction. (See ***Fresnel Lens***) B-6, DE-5

Dipsey Lead (also *Dipsy Lead*) A heavy deep-water hand lead and its gear, for sounding. (e. XVII p.e.) The word is simply a corruption of deep-sea. DE-3

Ditty Bag A small bag in which a sailor keeps small tools and equipment, also small personal articles. (Possibly XVII) The origin is not certain. It may have been from Hindi for a type of cloth, from *dittis*, a kind of tobacco, or it could go back to Anglo-Saxon—*dite*, tidy. (I like this one.) L-8, DE-3

Ditty Box is a variation in shape, but not in purpose, of the ditty bag, that was created by Navy sailors; a miniature sea chest. (m. XIX) L-8, DE-3

Dock is a term often used too loosely. Properly it is the waterspace between piers, or a basin or other device by which a vessel can be taken out of the water. (XIV) The term comes from Middle Dutch, *docke*, of these meanings. M-2, WO-1, WS-1

Dodger In modern parlance, any of several devices, usually of cloth, to protect the sailor from wind and spray, in large vessels and small. (XIX p.e.) The word itself comes from the Scottish *dodd*, dodge, and was seen in the XVI century. (See ***Weathercloth, Pavisade***) DE-3

Dog The name for a lever to close or tighten a hatch or door. A dog has been a part of a lock or latch, from the XV. When it began to pertain to ships is not certain (possibly XVI). DE-3

Dog-and-Bitch Thimble A specially shaped thimble to allow a block to be brought closer in to a fitting. The term was seen in the XIX century; but the device goes back to the days of spritsails. The origin is uncertain, but clearly implies a close connection. L-6

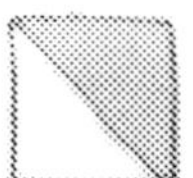

Dog House (also *Doghouse*) A low deckhouse. (XIX p.e.) It is believed originally to have been a temporary small, low structure to accommodate personnel when a vessel was overcrowded, possibly in the days of the slavers. H-2

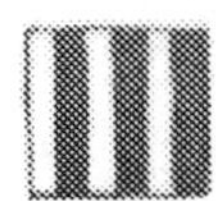

Dog Vane A weather vane or telltale, mounted in the view of the helmsman and of the officer of the watch of a sailing vessel; an old term but still sometimes heard. (e. XVII p.e.) Earlier fane, vane comes from the Anglo-Saxon *fana*, flag. The connection of dog is not clear. M-2, DE-5

Dog Watch A two-hour watch, 1600-1800 and 1800-2000; a long-standing practice followed when it is desirable to have the crew change the times of their watches every day. (XVI) The origin is not certain, but a good guess is that they were once called curtailed watches (which they were), this slid to docked, and that in turn to dog. WM-3a

Doldrums The belt around the world near the equator where much calm weather is encountered. (XIX p.e.) One scholar conjectures that this was a slang word, made-up of dumps and tantrums. WW-1

Dolphin A pile, usually made up of several heavy stakes or beams driven into the bottom, in a harbor, to which a vessel can moor. (XVIII) The origin can only be guessed at—that some early ones were highly decorated, probably with dolphins. DE-3

Dolphin Striker A nickname for the martingale boom on a sailing vessel. The word probably came into being, as did the spar, late in the XVIII century. S-3

Donkey The donkey boiler and donkey engine, in the early days of steam, were for all kinds of heavy hauling, to reduce the need for manpower, in sailing ships. It appears to be a slang term. (m. XIX) Small boilers for auxiliary steam on modern ships are called donkey boilers. S-3, DE-3

Donkey's Breakfast A sailor's nickname for a straw mattress, issued in some forecastles in the early XIX century. K-1

Dorade Ventilator A type of small-craft deck ventilator designed to admit air but not water below. It was named for a famous racing yacht, the yawl *Dorade*, designed by Olin Stephens in 1929. The ventilator was designed by Roderick Stephens in 1933. R-2

Dory A general type of multipurpose pulling and sailing boat, used extensively for offshore fishing in Northeastern waters. (XVIII) This very seaworthy craft, of simple and sturdy straight-sided construction, with much sheer and raked ends, is believed to have been developed by our French explorers, its predecessor being the *bateau* (which see). One source says the term came from *dorée*, a French word for gilded, which dories are not. *Orée (d'orée)* means the edge of a forest or woods. As a source of wood and a place to build a boat, this makes good sense. B-6, DE-5, WAB, JG, JR

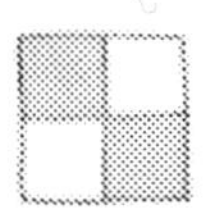

Double A verb, to make a passage around a point, cape or peninsula, i.e., "The Cape." (XVI) The origin in this sense is obscure. B-6, DE-5, WAB

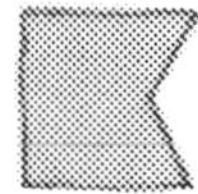

Doubling The name given to the section aloft, in which a lower and upper mast overlap. (XVII) B-6, DE-3

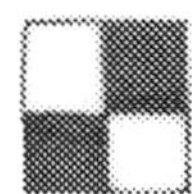

Douse (also *Dowse*) To take down, as a sail. (XVII) Also to put out, as a lamp or light. It comes from both Dutch and German, *dossen*, of the same meaning. WO-1

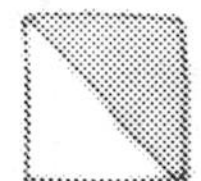

Down East Anyone who isn't familiar with the Maine Coast and its waters may ask, "why 'down'?" Two possible answers: one is that no matter where one is in New England, one always goes "up" to Boston. Another is that to sail across the Gulf of Maine, as to Nova Scotia, the magnetic course is south of east. A possible third explanation is that one sailed downwind all the way, but I would suggest not counting on this. JR, WM-3

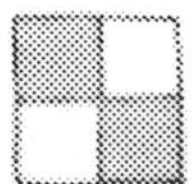

Down Easter (also *Downeaster*) Any large wooden sailing ship built in Maine, from about the end of the Civil War to the early XX century. The latter-day vessels were mostly coasting schooners, but the earlier ones were square-riggers: ships, barks, and barkentines. C-1, KK

Drabler (also *Drabbler*) A second bonnet on a sail. (XIV) The word came from the Middle English *drabblen*, to get wet, or splash. (See *Bonnet*) S-2, DE-3

Draft (also *Draught*) The underwater vertical dimension of a craft, "the depthe of water she requireth so as not to touch the bottome." (e. XVII p.e.) The word comes from late Middle English, and possibly goes back to Old German. M-2, DE-3

Draw (1) A vessel is said to draw however many feet of water that are her draft. (XVI) The origin of the word in this sense is obscure. W-2, DE-5 (2) Of a sail, that it is "full," and doing its job. (XVII p.e.) In this meaning the word goes back to Old Norse, thence to Old English, *dragen*, to pull. S-2, DE-3

Dredge (1) To dig out or deepen a channel. (2) A vessel that does the dredging. (3) Dragging an anchor on purpose. (See *Clubbing*) (e. XVII p.e.) The term probably comes in all these meanings from the Anglo-Saxon ***drecq***, to draw or pull. M-2, WS-1

Dress Ship, To To decorate a vessel for a special celebration. This customarily is done by stringing signal flags from the bow, over the mastheads and down to the stern. (XVIII p.e.) The custom was naval in origin. F-1b, L-8

Drogue A sea anchor. The word is related, aptly enough, to drag, and appears to come from early German. My sources say XIX, but I am confident that drogues were so used, and so named, long before then. WO-1, DE-5

Drop with its many meanings, is the name for the vertical measure, usually at the center, of a square sail. (XVIII p.e.)The word in this sense comes from Old English, ***dropian***, meaning distance downward. DE-3

Drop Keel (also *Dropkeel*) (See *Centerboard*). B-6, WAB

Drydock Broadly, any device that takes a ship out of her element. The oldest type for larger ships is a graving dock. A modern type is a barge-like vessel which can be flooded and lowered, a ship moved in, the dock pumped out, lifting the ''patient'' high-and-dry. The graving dock dates from the XVI century; the new, called a floating drydock, from the XIX. (See *Camel, Graving Dock*) S-2

Dubbing The almost-lost art of shaping and smoothing a vessel's timbers with an adze. (XV p.e.) The term is very probably derived from the Anglo-Saxon word ***dubbon***, meaning light stroke. WS-1

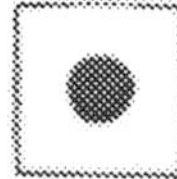

Duck High quality cotton canvas cloth, in heavier grades for sails, lighter for clothing. (XVI) Earlier, the term applied to flax cloth, i.e., linen. It appeared in Middle English as ***dock***, of the same meaning; and similar words were seen in the Nordics. WS-1

Duffle A name given to a sailor's personal effects. Also spelled ***duffel***, it referred to his principal clothing, also to the seabag in which he carried and stowed it. The term comes from the Flemish town of Duffel near Antwerp, and denotes a rough woolen cloth made there. WS-1

Dungarees The modern sailor's work clothes. The term is not modern, however. It is XVIII century, and comes from the Hindi word ***dungri***, for a type of Indian cotton cloth. WM-3, DE-4

Dunnage Light, usually scrap, timber used to chock or brace cargo and stores in a ship's hold. Earlier, it was often spelled ***dinnage***. (XIV) The term came from Middle Dutch, ***dunne***, a collection of light material. WO-1, DE-4

Dutchman A small patch, usually of wood, to repair damage or replace rotted material. (XVIII p.e.) The word is considered to be pure slang. DE-3

Earing A line used in bending a sail to a spar; also the line passed through the cringles when reefing a square sail. (e. XVII p.e.) Earlier, the spelling was ear-ring. The origin of the term is obscure; it could have been a nickname. S-2

Easting Distance sailed eastward. (XVII, p.e.) On the long eastward leg for ships sailing for Australia via the Cape of Good Hope, or from Australia via "The Horn" for the North Atlantic, a ship was said to "run her easting down." K-1, V-1a, DE-3

Ebb Outgoing tidal flow. (XVI) The word came from Anglo-Saxon, *ebba*, coming to us via Old English, French, and Middle English. WO-1

Eddy A circular or reverse flow of current. (XII) The Middle English word was *ydy*; it came from Icelandic, also perhaps from the Anglo-Saxon *ed*, backwards. WO-1

Embark To go aboard a vessel, especially at the outset of a voyage or cruise. (XVI) It came from the French *embarquer*, and goes back to the Latin *imbarcare*, to put in a ship. WO-1

Engine is an older word than we normally think of it. (XV) Before the coming of steam and other power, it meant any mechanical device, usually complicated, to achieve a physical function. The word comes from the Latin *ingenium*, meaning natural capacity. WS-1, DE-4

Ensign (1) A national flag. In this sense, the word came, via French *ensigne*, from Latin *insignia*, badge. (XVI) (2) The lowest commissioned rank in the Navy and Coast Guard. The term in this sense was adopted from the British and French, in whose armies this was, and is, a special junior officer's rank. WS-1

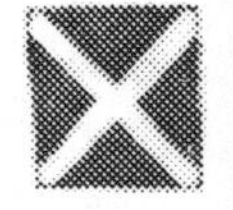

Ephemeris An astronomical almanac containing data on celestial bodies. (XVII) The word came, via Latin, from the Greek, same word and same meaning. The first of such studies are believed to have been done in ancient Greece. B-6, WO-1

Euphroe A deadeye with many holes, used to rig an old-style crowfoot. (XVII p.e.) The word has several spellings; it came from Middle Dutch, *juffreuw*, of the same meaning. A-2, WO-1

Eyebrow A metal ridge, usually curved and earlier of wood, over an air port, to shed water. (XVIII p.e.) On British ships it is usually called a *rigol*, which see. K-1, JR

Eyes The extreme bow. (XVI) Its origin is uncertain; it could refer to the eyes on the dragonheads usually seen on the bows of Viking ships of the Xth to XIIth centuries, or to the eyes on later figureheads, or to "the eye of the wind." M-2, DE-3

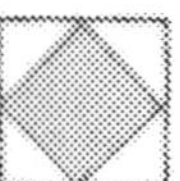

Fag End The end of a rope that has come unlaid. (XVIII p.e.) Also known as a cow's tail or a deadman. The word probably came from Middle English, *flokken*, to flap about. F-1b, WS-1

Fairlead Any of several devices to control the lead, or direction, of a line. (Possibly XII) Fair and lead came from Old English. A-2, DE-4

Fake (1) One turn in a coil of rope. (2) A verb, to lay out line or chain on deck, for easy running or inspection.

There are different opinions on the term: some say the right word is *flake*, with which I disagree. Both of these words are used, however, and appear to be interchangeable. Fake was seen in the XVII century and probably earlier, as it came from Middle English *faken*, coil. M-2, S-2, DE-5

Fall The hauling part of a tackle. (XVII p.e.) This term came from Middle English, *fallen*, fall, one meaning of which was in this sense. The tackles on boat davits, also the modern single wire cables, are called boat-falls. M-2, DE-4

Fancy Line Also one word, a type of downhaul for a fore-and-aft sail, earlier for overhauling a lee topping lift on a square-rigger. (XVII p.e.) An old meaning of fancy was extra. S-3, DE-3

Fantail The aftermost part of a ship usually of the main deck; at the extreme stern. This word is believed to be purely American, from the early days of elyptical (fan-shaped) sterns, the mid-XIX. M-1, N-4, JR

Fardage An old word for dunnage, especially applying to bulk cargo. (XIV p.e.) The term comes, via Middle English, from Old English, *fardel*, bundle, and goes back to Arabic, *fardah*, load or bundle. DE-3

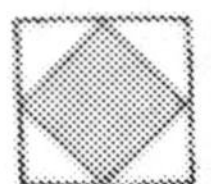

Farthel An old word for furl, particularly for the courses and spritsail. (e. XVII p.e.) It could have the same derivation as fardage, or that of furl. K-1, M-2

Fashion Piece A timber or plate that is part of the form of the stern, to which the ends of a square transom are attached. (e. XVII p.e.) The origin of the term is obscure. S-2, WAB

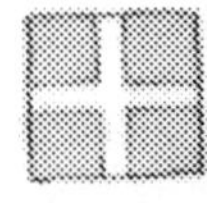

Fast Secure, securely belayed or tied. (e. XVII p.e.) The word came from Anglo-Saxon, same word and meaning, whether in the nautical sense is likely but not certain. S-2, WS-1

Fastening Pertaining to a vessel's construction, the method by which her planks or plates are fastened to the frames. (XIII) The word comes from the Old English *faestnian*, fasten, possibly in the nautical sense. S-2, WS-1

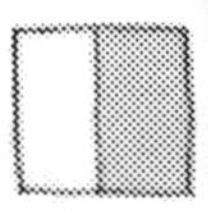

Fathom The mariner's unit of measure, six feet. The term came from the Anglo-Saxon word *foethm*, meaning the space reached by the fully extended arms (a method used today as a rough measure of a line), and also to embrace. It came into English probably in the XII century as *fadme*, and was seen in its present form in the XVI. S-2, WS-1

Fay To join, as in a ship's timbers, implying precision and strength. (XVIII p.e.) The term appears to be an old one, possibly from Middle English, *fegen*, to fit. DE-3, DE-4

Feaze (also *Fease*) To fray out rope to get rope yarn. (XIV) A similar word was seen in Middle Dutch, but the origin is more likely Old English, *faes*, fringe. S-2, DE-3

Felloe The outer edge of a ship's wheel; also the segments from which one was made. (XVII) The word comes from Old English, *felge*, of the latter meaning. S-3, DE-4

Fender One of several devices for protecting the side of a boat or ship. (XIII p.e.) The term could be an aphetic of the Middle English word *defenden*, which came via Old English from Latin, *defendere*, defend or protect. Fenders on ships of earlier days (about XV to XVII centuries) were part of their hull; they were exterior timbers parallel to the frames. S-1, WS-1

One sailor's definition of a yacht fender is one that is over the side only when needed, while a bumper is left hanging out when under way. The latter term and practice are considered lubberly by some.

Ferrule (also *Ferral*) A band, usually of iron, to strengthen a spar. (XVI) This term comes from Old French, *viral*, of the same general meaning. WS-1

Ferry Any craft that makes a short and regular passage from one point to another. (XII) The word goes back to Anglo-Saxon, *ferian*, of the same meaning. WS-1

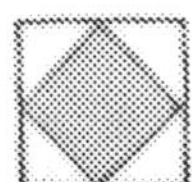

Fetch (1) To arrive at a desired point. (XVI p.e.) The origin in this meaning is Old English, *feccon*, achieve. DE-3 (2) An old word for a tack or a reach. (XVI) The derivation in this sense is obscure. W-2 (3) An expanse of water, such as the extent of a bay or a coastline indentation. (XIX p.e.) S-3, DE-3 (4) The distance through which a wave or wind system on a body of water advances. (XIX) DE-3 The word in these two meanings appears to have come from Old English, *fetian*, to reach. DE-3 (5) Of a vessel, to gain motion ahead or astern. (XVII) S-2, DE-3 (6) To prime a pump. (XVIII p.e.) F-1, DE-3 In these two senses the origin is obscure.

Fetch Way, To An old term for a mast that has become unstable at deck level, usually from the working-loose of its wedges. (XVII p.e.) Its origin is Old French, *fiche*, fix. S-2, DE-5

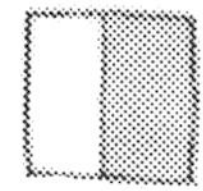

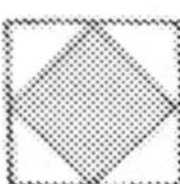

Fid (1) an elongated conical hardwood tool for rope working. (e. XVII p.e.) (See *Marlinspike*) M-2, WW-1 (2) A wood or metal pin passing through the heel of an upper mast, resting on the trestletree of its lower mast. (e. XVII p.e.) M-2, DE-3 The origin of both meanings is obscure; it could have come from the Latin word *figgare*, to drive in or fix.

Fiddle A rack or rail on the edge of a table, dresser, counter, or stove; to keep dishes, cookpots, etc., in place in rough seas. (e. XVII p.e.) The term very probably originated from the fact that early fiddles often were little stanchions with light lines stretched taut between them like fiddle strings. WW-1, DE-3

Fiddle Board An adjustable or detachable board, serving the same purpose as a fiddle. (XIX) The origin seems apparent. M-1

Fiddleheads Ornamental timbers at the beakhead. (XVII) The name came from the fact that they were curved in the general shape of the head of a fiddle. K-1, DE-5

Fiddler's Green is the old name for the seaman's heaven, where the grass is green, fiddlers play, wine flows, and "mates not permitted." (XVII p.e.) H-2, T-1

Fiddley A grating over the machinery spaces of a steamship, and later on a motorship. (1. XIX) The origin of the term is not known. K-1

Field Day A day, or a few hours, set aside for cleaning up on deck and below. The term was undoubtedly originated by navy people, who enjoyed nothing more than scrubbing the decks and paintwork, shining the brass, etc., sometimes to get ready for an inspection. Now in fairly general use, the term appeared during or shortly after World War I. N-4

Fife Rail A heavily braced rail structure, usually at the foot of a mast, on deck, for belaying lines. (XVII p.e.) The origin can only be guessed at, that fife may have been a nickname for a belaying pin. DE-3

Figurehead A statue-like symbolic ornament at the stem of a ship. Bow ornamentation has been a custom in many areas and for many centuries. Generally those under this definition came into fashion in about the XVI century, and, sadly, began disappearing in the early XX. K-1

Fish (1) A splint for a broken or damaged spar. (2) To repair a spar with a fish. (Both e. XVII p.e.) The derivation in these meanings is Old French, *fiche*, to fix. (3) To bring an anchor ''home'' when hoisting, to secure it for sea. (e. XVII p.e.) In this sense the origin is obscure. S-2, DE-5

Fix A well-established position of a ship at sea, in navigation. The term appeared with this meaning in the XVI century, however with a far lesser degree of accuracy than at present. The origin is Old French, *fix*, of the same meaning. WO-1

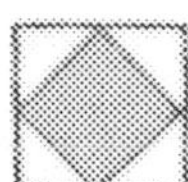

Flake See *Fake*.

Flank Speed Maximum possible speed. This term is mainly naval, and probably originated with our destroyers before or during World War I. It was the speed required to get to a new position in a formation or convoy in the shortest possible time, also to outflank enemy ships. N-4, JR

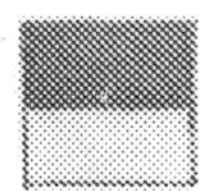

Fleet A large body or group of ships. This term was in use in the time of Sir Francis Drake (XVI). It comes from the Anglo-Saxon *fleot*, for fleet, and is seen in many languages in recognizable form. WO-1

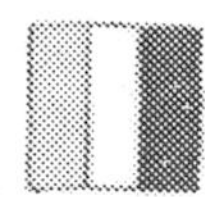

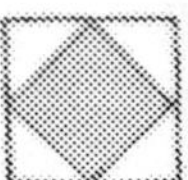

Flemish (1) A general descriptive word relating to gear and procedures emanating from The Netherlands and Belgium, whence came many that were adopted by the British. WW-1 (2) A short name for a Flemish coil, a flat ornamental coil of line; also a verb for doing one. (XVI) WW-1

Flemish Horse A footrope at the extreme end of a yard on a square-rigger. (XVII p.e.) Horse was an early term for a footrope, and these are believed first to have been in use in Dutch ships. (See *Horse*)

Flinders Bar A bar of soft iron used in compensating a magnetic compass, to reduce the deviation when a vessel rolls or heels. It was named for its inventor, Nathaniel Flinders, a renowned British explorer and scientist (1774-1814). DE-1

Floor A 'thwartship, or transverse, structural member of a hull, just above the keel or keelson, to hold the frames in place. (e. XVII p.e.) The word comes from Old Norse, *flor*, and may have applied to later Viking-type ships (the earlier ones did not have floors as such). S-2, DE-3

Flotilla A small group of ships. (XVII p.e.) The word comes directly from Spanish, and means a small fleet. WO-1

Fluke A blade of an anchor, also called a palm (e. XVII p.e.) The word probably came, via Middle English, from the Old English *floc*, which also meant the fluke of a fish. M-2, DE-4

Flying (1) Anything high in a ship, as a flying jib, or flying bridge. The term was in use in the XVII century, applying particularly to rigging. (2) To hoist a sail or flag free of stops. The dating in this sense is uncertain; probably XVIII. M-2, DE-3

Footrope A fixed line suspended under a yard or the bowsprit of a sailing ship, for use as the name implies. The gear came into use gradually, starting, it is believed, in the XVI century, and probably first was used by the Dutch. They were not in common use before the mid-XVII. (One marvels at what sailors could do aloft before that time.) (See *Horse*) A-2, WAB

Fore- Anything forward, as a prefix. (XV p.e.) Its origin is Anglo-Saxon, same word and same meaning. S-1, WS-1

Fore-and-Aft is the name of a vessel's rig, also of her sails, when the plane of the sails is basically on the centerline. (e. XVIII) The first of such modern rigs were seen in Dutch waters in late XVI. The concept goes back several centuries further. (See *Lateen*) T-1, WAB

Forecastle (Often abbreviated to Fo'c's'l and pronounced that way.) Now simply the foredeck of a ship or boat, this term formerly meant a raised platform at the bow, often armored, for archers and, later, musketeers. (XIII) In the XVII to XX centuries, in many ships it was the location, ergo the name, of the crew's quarters. (One oldtimer is quoted as saying, "and it wasn't no castle.") (See *Pavisade*) WS-1

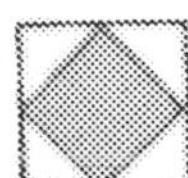

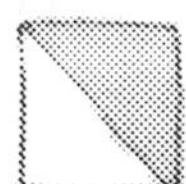

Forefoot The part of the hull where the stem joins the keel. (XV p.e.) The word comes from Middle English, *forfot*, of the same meaning. M-2, DE-4

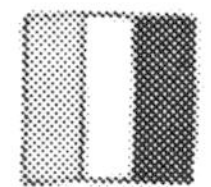

Foreganger (See *Bending Shot*) (XVIII p.e.) This appears to be more of a British term than American, and comes from the Dutch *voorganger* or German *vorganger*, possibly both, and both meaning the same thing. DE-3

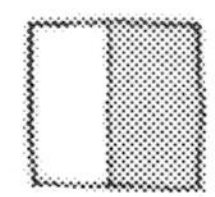

Fother To make or apply a collision mat, and a name for the materials from which one is made. (XVII p.e.) The term comes from Anglo-Saxon, *foden*, stuffing. DE-3

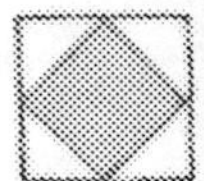

Found Generally with a qualifying word, such as "well" or "poorly" (also "singly" if a vessel only had one of everything), it refers to the quality and quantity of her gear. (XVIII p.e.) The term comes from an old meaning of the word find, which was to provide; from the Old English *finden*, of this meaning. WO-1, DE-3

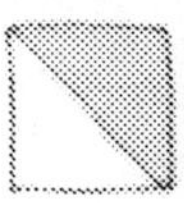

Founder The unwelcome term for sinking from damage; usually from overwhelming sea conditions. (e. XVII p.e.) This term comes from Middle English, *foundren*, in turn from Old French, *effondrir*, to engulf or sink. S-2, WS-1

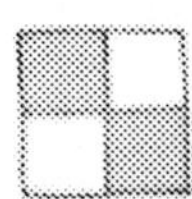

Fox Twisted or braided ropeyarn for making grommets, strops, etc. (XVIII) Its origin is obscure; it is possibly a nickname. F-1, DE-3

Frames are the "ribs," and sometimes called that, of any craft. (e. XVII p.e., possibly XIV or even earlier.) The word comes from Old Italian, *fram*, frame, but it is uncertain that it was used at that time in the nautical sense. DE-3

Frap To wrap two or more lines together, for various purposes. (XIV) It comes from Old English, and from Old French; the latter, *fraper*, to wrap. WO-1

Freeboard The height of a craft's side above the waterline. (XIV) Its origin is Anglo-Saxon, *framebord*, frames' side. DE-3

Freshen (1) To freshen the nip, or the hawse, is to render, or haul in a line to change its position in a block, fairlead or hawsehole, to protect it against chafe. (2) To freshen ballast is to alter its location for better trim. (Both e. XVII p.e.) The derivation in these senses is not known. The word itself comes from Old French. B-1, DE-3

Fresnel Lens The multiple-facet lens of many uses, such as for lighthouses, light buoys, and a ship's running lights, to control focus and amplify light beams. It was named after Augustin Jean Fresnel, a noted French physicist (1788-1827). DE-1

Frigate In sailing ship days, a fast mid-sized ship-rigged warship, with one or two gun decks. (XVII) In World War II, a junior-grade destroyer-type; more recently the term designating a large destroyer or a destroyer-leader. The term comes from the Old French *fregate*, the precise meaning of which appears obscure. WO-1

Funnel Earlier, a steamship's smokestack for her boilers; now an exhaust stack for any machinery-driven vessel. (XIX) The term possibly came into being as the early types sometimes looked like an inverted funnel. (See *Stack*) WO-1, JR

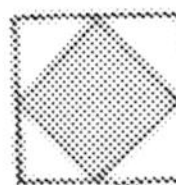

Furl To fold or roll a sail on its yard or boom. (e. XVII p.e.) Earlier terms were *furdle* and *farthel*. It comes from French, and this from Old French, *ferlier*, to bind; and could have had its origin in Arabic. S-2, WS-1

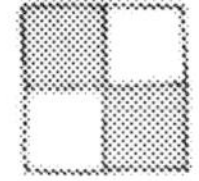

Futtock Part of a made-up frame of a wooden ship. (XIII) The word is a corruption of foot-hook, and comes from *futtaker*, Middle English of this meaning. WO-1, WS-1

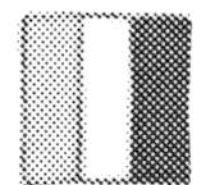

Futtock Shrouds Short sections of cable or rod in square-riggers, to stay the tops. They had ratlines for the seamen to achieve the next ''level'' aloft. (m. XIII p.e.) The origin as the same as for futtock frames, and foot-hooks they were. (See *Tops, The*) S-2, T-1

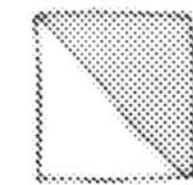

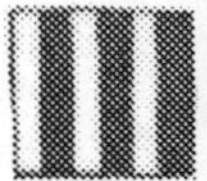

Gaff The upper spar of a fore-and-aft, four-sided sail, the first of which, in larger craft, was the fore-and-aft spanker that was replacing the lateen sail in the XVIII century. The origin is obscure in its present meaning, but the word comes from Old French, *gaffe*, gaff or cudgel. WO-1, WS-1

Gale A continuous strong wind, of about thirty-five to sixty-five knots in velocity. (XVI p.e.) The derivation is uncertain; it could be from Old Norse, *gallen*, meaning mad, or frantic. WO-1

***Galiot** (also Galliot)* A small, fast galley seen mostly in the Mediterranean Sea. (XVII-XVIII) The term comes from the French *galiote*, a diminutive for *galie*, which in turn comes from Old French. (See *Galley, Galleon*) WO-1

Gall An old word for that mighty enemy of the mariner, chafe. (e. XVII p.e.) This one goes back to the Anglo-Saxon *gealle*, chafe. S-2, DE-3

Gallant (See *Topgallant*)

Galleas A fighting galley. (XV to XVIII) This word came from Old French, via modern, *galleasse*, of this same meaning. (See *Galley*) L-1, DE-4

Galleon The typical large sailing ship of XVI to XVIII centuries; very curvy, with a high poop and after-structure, a high forecastle and pronounced beakhead. The term comes Old French, *galion*, and goes back to Latin, *galea*, galley. WO-1

Galley (1) A fighting vessel, propelled with oars, perhaps up to thirty to a side, often in tiers; sometimes with sail as auxiliary power. (XIII) The word goes back, via Old French, to the Latin *galea*, as for the derivation of galleon, and can be traced to Greek. WO-1 (2) A ship's kitchen. (p. XVIII) The term's origin in this sense is not certain. A good guess is that the cook and his helpers were considered, or considered themselves, galley slaves. JR

Gallows A fixed frame to support a spar or spars when not in use. (e. XVII p.e.) The word came from Middle English, *galwes*, and is from the Anglo-Saxon *galgas*, gibbet. WO-1

Gam A sailor's "bull session." Earlier, a chat or conference among whaleships' captains, ashore or more often at sea. (XVIII or XIX) The best guess on the origin of this term is that it was a whaleman's slang word for a pod of whales. DE-4

Gammoning The lashing that held the bowsprit of a sailing ship in place at the stem, before being replaced with iron. (XVI p.e.) The origin is Old French, *gambon*, gammon, and possibly alludes to tying up a ham. A-2

Gammon Iron The iron band that replaced gammoning (whence its origin) to hold the bowsprit in place. (XIX) C-1a

Gangplank The bridge-like structure for access to the shore, when a ship is docked. (XVII p.e.) Gang comes unchanged from Anglo-Saxon, then meaning path or course. Plank comes from Middle English, *planke*, board. (See *Brow*) DE-3

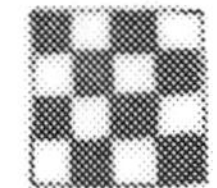

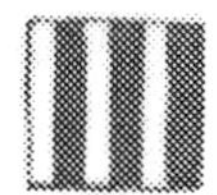

Gangway (1) One word for a passageway aboard a ship. (2) An opening for access to or from a ship. (3) Another word for gangplank. Way comes from the Anglo-Saxon *weg*, way. (In all senses XVII p.e.) S-2, WS-1

Gantline (See *Girtline*)

Garboard The lowest strake on a vessel's hull, that abuts the keel. (e. XVII p.e.) Earlier gorboard, the word comes from the Dutch *gaarboard*, of this same meaning. (See *Strake*) S-2, WO-1

Garland (1) A fixed strop around a mast. (2) A strop used for hoisting spars into place aloft. (Both XV) This term came from Middle English, *garlande*, of this general meaning, and may have come from Old French. S-1, WO-1

Garnet (1) A tackle on a square-rigger, usually rigged from a yard's end, for handling stores and cargo. (2) A clew line for the courses on a square-rigger; also called a clew garnet. (e. XVII p.e. for both) The derivation is Old French, *garant*, a fall tackle. S-2, WW-1

Gaskets Short lines, or lengths of sennit or cloth, used for furling sails, also awnings, boat covers, etc. (XVII p.e.) Earlier they were called caskets. The term probably comes from the French *garcette*, meaning a plait of rope. S-2, DE-4

Gear An all-encompassing word for a ship's or sailor's equipment, large and small, simple and sophisticated. (XV) It came from Middle English, *gere*, thence from Icelandic, *gervi*, both words having the same meaning. S-1, WS-1

Genoa Jib A large overlapping jib on a sailing yacht. (e. XX) Conceived by a well-known Swedish racing skipper, Sven Salen, the "jennie" (its much-used nickname) first appeared in the U.S. in 1927. The name was inspired by the large jibs seen for many years in the region of Genoa, Italy. R-2

Gig has had several definitions over the years; now probably best known as the name given to the boat assigned to the commanding officer of a larger naval vessel. (XVIII p.e.) The word came from the Middle English *gigge*, small boat. WS-1

Gilguy (1) A temporary guy, stay, or preventer. (2) Also a word for any gear or device the name of which doesn't come to mind at the moment. (XVIII p.e.) The origin of the word is uncertain but appears to be from Scottish. S-3, DE-3

Gimbals (1) A system of concentric rings on hinges. or (2) A one-plane system of hinges, to keep equipment fairly level when a vessel rolls or heels. (e. XVII p.e.) Earlier the term applied only to the compass, and earlier words were gimmels, and gemmon. This term probably relates to the Middle French *gemeau*, twin, which in turn goes back to Latin, *gemmelus*, twin. WS-1

Gimlet (also *Gimbet*) To turn an anchor, when heading for sea. (p. XV) Its origin perhaps is a Norman dialect word *guinblet*, to turn. WS-1

Gin Block A large block, usually with open cheeks made of metal, for handling heavy gear and cargo. The term dates from the XV century, but no doubt with a different definition. It came from Middle English, the same word, and possibly a corruption of the Old French word *engin*. (See *Engine*) DE-3

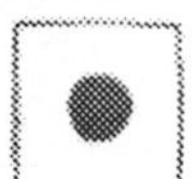

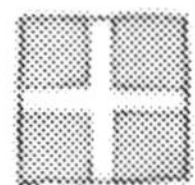

Gipsy (also *Gypsy*, etc.) The warping head of a winch or windlass. (XIX) The origin of the term is not known. DE-3

Girtline (also *Gantline*) A light tackle to handle sails, gear, or a man aloft in a boatswain's chair. (p. XVI) The term is now rare. Its origin is obscure; it appears to be a corruption of girth. F-1b, WO-1

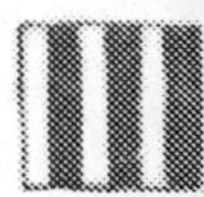

Glim A candle or lantern once used in a ship's crew quarters; now slang for any light. (XVII p.e.) It is said to be early Modern English cant. DE-3

Glory Hole Earlier, a holding cell for prisoners. In the late XIX and early XX centuries it was the name given to the stewards' quarters on a passenger ship. The origin is not known, but it appears to be another example of seamen's whimsy—glorious neither was. WO-1, JR

Gob A slang word for lower-rated enlisted men in the Navy (and one they do not like). (e. XX) The derivation is not known. It may have reference for the renowned ability of the young Navy man to gobble his chow. N-4, WM-1

Golliwobbler The nickname given to a large main staysail used by a schooner in light winds. (1. XIX or e. XX) It probably comes from goliwog, a slang word for something grotesque. DE-5, JR

Gondola The famed oar-propelled boat of the canals of Venice. (1. XVI) A generic word, it possibly is related to the Greek *kondy*, a drinking vessel. The Assyrians had a similar craft (ca. VIII B.C.). WO-1

Gooseneck A device for securing a boom to its mast—a type of hinge. (XVIII p.e.) The term may have got its start as a nickname, referring to the flexibility of a goose's neck. U-1c

Gores are strips of cloth sewed together to make a sail. (e. XVII p.e.) This word goes back to Old English and Anglo-Saxon, both *gaga*, thence to Middle English, *gore*, all of the same meaning. M-2, WS-1

Grapnel A small, many-pronged (or fluked) anchor, also used for dragging the bottom as for objects lost overboard. (XVI) The term apparently comes from several sources in Northern Europe, one being Anglo-Saxon, *grapenal*, another Old French, *grapon*, grab, hold. S-2, W-2, WO-1

Grappling Iron (See *Grapnel*)

Grassline Another name for *Coir*. (XVIII p.e.) K-1

Grating A wooden or metal open-work platform or covering. (e. XVII p.e.) This word came, via Middle English, from the Latin *cratis*, wickerwork. S-2, DE-4

Graving Dock A fixed shoreside drydock. (XVI) One version of the origin is early modern English, ''that which is dug out,'' but it more likely has to do with the dock's function, a means of cleaning, i.e., greaving, a vessel's sides and bottom. (See *Greave*) DE-3

Graving Piece A shaped piece of wood to repair damage or rot, as to the decks, rails, etc. (p. XIV) The term's derivation is the Old English *grafen*, to dig or carve. DE-3

Greave (also *Grave*) A term for burning off foul matter from a ship's bottom. (e. XVII p.e.) Earlier it was to apply greave, a mixture of tallow and train oil, as a preservative and for anti-fouling (that ageless problem). The word comes from earlier English, apparently originating with the Anglo-Saxon *greofa*, of the same general meaning. S-2, WS-1

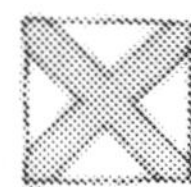

Gripe (1) An abnormal tendency for a sailing craft to turn into the wind. (XVII) (2) A strop, or other gear, to hold a ship's boat secure in its davits. (Also p. XVII, as this appears to be when the first davits were seen.) The word comes from Middle English, *gripan*, and it from Anglo-Saxon, the same word, both meaning to seize. S-2, WS-1

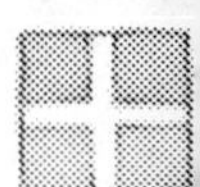

Grog A mixture of rum and water. Traditionally, until recently, it was rationed to enlisted men of the British and Commonwealth navies. (XVIII) It is believed to have been named after an Admiral Vernon, R.N., who affected jackets made of grogram and gave them good service, and whose "lower decks" nickname was "Old Grog." Admiral Vernon brought about the regulation to dilute the rum ration, which may have increased the efficacy of some R.N. people. WM-3

Grommet (1) A ring made of line, yarn, and more recently of metal, sewed into a sail for various purposes. (XV) (2) A "fancywork" handle or grip of a sailor's sea chest. (XVIII) (3) A "salty" word for the stiffener in the crown of a Service or merchant marine officer's peak cap. (XIX) The word comes from the Old French, *grommette*, chain, the nautical sense of which is obscure. WO-1

Ground The bottom. (XVI p.e.) It comes from the Old English *grund*, of the same meaning among many others. WO-1

Grow To lie or extend in a given direction, especially the anchor cable. (e. XVIII p.e.) This word comes, via Middle English, from Old English, *growan*, to tend in direction. F-1, DE-4

Gudgeon A socket on the sternpost, through which the pintle on the rudder fits, forming a hinge. (XIV) Scholars differ on its derivation, as it gets confused with gudgeon, the fish. It appears to come from the Middle

English *gudyon*, this from French, *goujon*, pin or tenon, and could go back to Latin and Greek (but not for stern rudders, as they did not have them). Earlier spellings gudion and gudjin. (See *Pintle*) S-2, WS-1

Guess Warp (also *Guest Warp, Guest Rope*) A line from forward on a ship, led to the end of a boat boom, thence to a boat. (e. XVII p.e.) The term came from the Middle English *gyeswarp*, of the same general meaning. (See *Painter*) M-2, DE-5

Gundalow In Europe, a ship's boat or small war vessel (XVII p.e.). In North America, a large, flat bottomed riverboat, sometimes used as a gunboat. (XVIII) The term could be a corruption of *gondola*. C-1d, DE-3, JG

Gunter Rig A sailboat rig; a triangular fore-and-aft sail, usually with a boom but always with a gaff peaked up so that it is virtually parallel with the mast. (XIX p.e.) It is believed to have been named for Edmund Gunter, a noted marine mathematician, but the connection seems obscure. DE-4

Gunwale The upper edge, or low bulwark on the side of a vessel. (XV) The definition has varied over the years with changes in ships' and boats' design. Earlier, and generally, it was the top of the bulwark structure, the guns being carried on the main deck. Often contracted to *gunnel*. (See *Wale*) S-2, WO-1

Guy A line or tackle to steady a sail, yard, or cargo boom. (e. XVII p.e.) The word comes from the Middle English *gye*, and it from Old French, *guie*, both meaning guide. S-2, WS-1

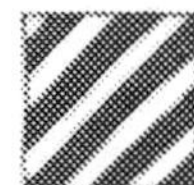

Gypsy (See *Gipsy*)

Hack Watch Any of a variety of good-quality watches, used in small vessels as a substitute for a chronometer, and on larger ones for keeping the time when taking sights or timed bearings. (XIX) The origin of the term is uncertain: it is probably a corruption of *hackney*, in the sense of ordinary. DE-3, JR

Hail (1) To call to another vessel, to call her people's attention, especially at sea. (XVI) The word comes, via Middle English, from Old Norse, *heill*, hail, welcome. (2) A vessel is said to hail from her home port. We have no specific data on this sense, but a guess is that when hailing at sea, a ship would usually identify herself by her name and home port. M-2, WS-1

Half-Deck A deck above the main deck, which does not run the full length of the vessel. The term usually refers to the later, larger square-riggers, and steamers, of the XIX century. However the term was seen earlier, i.e. (e. XVII p.e.) S-2

Half Seas Over (1) Past a point of no return. (m. XVI) (2) Drunk. (e. XVIII) WM-3

Halyard (also *Halliard*) A line on any craft, for hoisting sails, some spars, and flags. (XIII) This is a composite word, in effect "haul yard." Haul is from Old French, *haler*, and Old Saxon, *halar*, both meaning haul. Yard is from Old English and Old Saxon, *gerd*, for spar. S-2, WS-1, WO-1

Hamberline (also *Hambroline*) A strong, three-part small stuff for seizing, lacing sails, and lashing. (l. XVIII) A good guess is that the name is a corruption of Hamburg line. DE-5

Hammock A hanging bed, shipboard use being common particularly to warships from the late XVIII to the early XX century. It is believed to have been of West Indian origin, and the word from the Spanish *jamaca*, hanging bed. WO-1

Hand (1) An old term for furling and taking-in sail. (XVI p.e.) (2) A member of a vessel's crew. (XIII) The word comes intact from Old English and Old Saxon, and means an employed person. M-2, DE-3

Handsomely To move or act slowly, steadily, and carefully. (p. XVII p.e.) This word comes from Middle English, *handsom*, easy to handle. DE-4

Handy Billy (1) Any assisting device. It usually refers to a light tackle for a variety of uses. (Also called a watch tackle.) (p. XVI) A composite word, handy goes back to Anglo-Saxon, *gehende*, near at hand. Billy is an old Scottish word, still heard, for an assisting tool. WO-1 WW-1 (2) A small gasoline-powered portable pump for damage control and firefighting purposes, the name of which was borrowed from the old use. (e. XX)

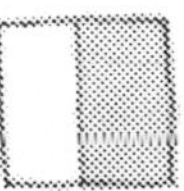

Hank A special hook, usually sewed or moused into the edge of a sail to fasten it to a stay or spar. (XIII) The term comes from Icelandic, *honk*, meaning hank, also *hanki*, a clasp, and possibly comes from Old German, *henken*, hang. S-1, WS-1

Happy Hour A short period of relaxation for all possible crew members. (e. XX) The term is believed to have originated in the Navy, about the time of World War I. N-4, DE-5

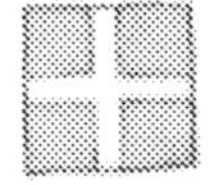

Harness Cask A cask or tub in which salted meat for the crew was kept. The name is a tribute to the meat's flavor and tenderness. (p. XVIII) B-1

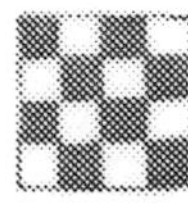

Harpings Any of a variety of especially strong wales on a wooden vessel, particularly at or near the bow. (e. XVII p.e.) The term probably comes from the French word *harpe*, a clamp, used in wall-building. M-2, WW-1

Harpoon A barbed spear for fishing and for whaling; also a verb referring to its use. An earlier term was harping iron. (XVI) The word may have been of Basque origin, as they were early whalers; or it may have come from the Dutch *harpoen*, of similar meaning. WO-1, WW-1

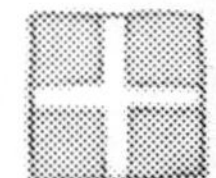

Hatch Any of a variety of shipboard openings, for personnel, gear, stores, and cargo. (XIII) The origin is uncertain, but it appears to be from Early English, *hacche*, which comes from Old English, *haec*, a gate, door, or grating. S-1, DE-3

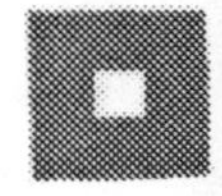

Haul (1) To pull, as on a line. (XVI) Earlier often spelled hall, the term comes from Old French, *hallier*, haul or pull. (2) Relating to the wind, a shift in direction, clockwise. (e. XVII p.e.) The origin in this sense is not clear. (See *Veer*) (3) To haul out, to take a craft out of the water. (4) To haul her wind was for a square-rigger to sail closer to the wind. (p. XIV) S-2, WO-1, DE-3

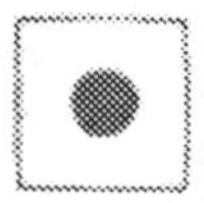

Hawse There are several uses for this term, but it generally pertains to the area in the bows, outboard under the bows, to anchoring and to mooring. (XIV) Earlier it was seen often as halse. The term was very generally Nordic, but was also seen in French. The Middle English *hale*, pertaining to the bows, was found in Old Norse and Icelandic, and appeared as *heals* in Old English and in Anglo-Saxon. S-1, WO-1

Hawser The heavy, cable-laid line for an anchor, and also used for towing, in earlier days. (XIV) In modern language it usually means a mooring line. As in the case for hawse, there were several different spellings. It came from Middle English, and thence from Anglo-Norman, ***haucer***, heavy rope. S-2, WO-1

Head The topmost or forward-most part of a vessel or of a component such as the stem, masthead, beakhead, rudder-head, and, later, the uppermost part or side of a sail. (XV p.e.) The origin of the word in these meanings is debatable; it probably comes from the Middle English suffix ***hede***, which goes back to Old English, ***heden***, head. S-1, WO-1

Head, The (also ***The Heads***) Earlier, the crew's latrine, now generally all the shipboard "facilities." The crew was traditionally quartered in the forecastle, immediately forward of which was the beakhead, on which the latrines were located, conveniently overhanging the water. (At times they were well washed down!) It is not known when the contraction to the word head became common. B-1

Headsail A sail carried forward, such as a jib, fore staysail, or earlier, a spritsail. (e. XVII p.e.) M-2

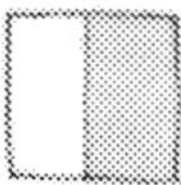

Heave To pull on a line. (e. XVII p.e.) This word came from the Anglo-Saxon ***hebban***, pull or heave. M-2, WO-1

Heel For a vessel or boat to lean over from the force of the wind. (XVI) The origin is the Anglo-Saxon word ***hieldan***, of this same meaning. M-2, WO-1

Helm The simplest definition is "tiller," but the term could be said to refer to the steering apparatus of any craft. (XVIII p.e.) There are several words from which the term could have been derived, one of which is the Old Norse ***hjalmvoh***, meaning rudder-handle. S-1, WO-1

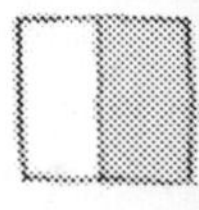

Hemp The tough fiber of the hemp plant, from which cordage and the thread for sails were made for many years. (XIII) The word comes from Old English, *hanap*, of the same meaning. WO-1

Hermaphrodite Brig A two-masted sailing vessel, one definition of which was that the foremast was square-rigged, the mainmast having a fore-and-aft mainsail, the topsail and all above it being square. (XVIII) The origin of the word in this sense has not been determined, but the inference is clear. T-1, WS-1

High and Dry An everyday shoreside term now, it was a sailor's expression, and this state of affairs was rarely intentional. (XVII p.e.) The definition seems obvious. WO-1

Hitch (1) A period of duty, long or short, such as a hitch at the wheel—one or two hours—or a four-year hitch in the Navy. (e. XVII p.e.) The term comes from Middle English, *hytchen*, of the same meaning. M-2, DE-3 (2) A type of knot. (XVI) The word in this sense comes from the Middle English *icche*, to catch. S-1, WO-1 (3) Another name for a tack, usually meaning a short one. (XIX p.e.) In this sense the origin is most likely the same as for the first. JR

Hog (1) Said of a craft that has lost her sheer, sagging downwards at her ends; said of any tired or badly built craft. (XVII) (2) A large heavy brush, or more recently a scraper, for bottom work. (XVIII p.e.) The background for the term in both meanings is not certain. For the first sense it may well have been a nickname, based on the graceless curve of a hogback. DE-3

Hoist To raise up, or lift. (XVI) Earlier, hoise, the word appears to have come from early Duch, *hyssen*, of the same meaning. S-2,WO-1

Hold A space in a vessel for cargo, and earlier for stores as well. (XV p.e.) This word comes, via Old English, from Old Norse, *hol*, meaning hollow. S-1, WO-1

Holiday A gap in one's shipboard work, as an unscrubbed or unpainted area. (XVIII) The origin is unknown; it may have reference to an unusual gap in work routine. DE-3, N-4

Holystone A block of sandstone, when last they were used (e. XX) for scouring decks. (XVIII) The origin of this term may be from the British Navy's people who were said to use blocks of gravestones, specifically those borrowed from a churchyard in Great Yarmouth, England. M-1

Home A general term used for gear when in its proper place, snug, or ready for sea. (e. XVII p.e.) The term comes from an Old English word *hom*, of this sense. M-2, DE-4

Honey Barge *(also Honey Boat)* A barge used for collecting trash and garbage from vessels ''anchored out'' in port. (p. l. XIX) It appears to be a typical navy sailor's nickname. N-4

Hooker Recently, a term describing any older vessel, originally it was a small two-masted craft of The Netherlands, usually a cargo boat. (XVII) The term comes from the Duch words *hoeker* and *hoekboot*, and very likely was related to The Hook. WO-1

Horns (1) Protrusions on the sides of a rudder to prevent its turning beyond an allowable angle. (XVII) (2) Outboard ends of the crosstrees and spreaders of a sailing ship. (e. XVII p.e.) The origin of the word in both senses is Old English and Old Norse, the same word, meaning horn-like. DE-3

Horse (1) A low iron or steel bar, parallel and fastened securely to the deck, along which the lower block of a fore-and-aft sail's sheet moves. It is also called a traveler. (XVII p.e.) S-2 (2) An older name for a footrope. (XVI) (See *Footrope*) A-2 (3) To pound, harden, or otherwise repair caulking, usually said "to horse up." (XVIII p.e.) K-1 The word comes, in all three senses, via Old English, from Old Norse, *hross*; these nautical connections to the quadruped are not clear. DE-4, S-2

Horse Latitudes Latitudes of about 30° to 35°North and South, in which the winds are usually light and capricious. (XVIII) There are several guesses as to the origin of this term. One was that horses on board were thrown overboard to save water; another was that it was taken from *El Golfo do las Yequas*, The Gulf of the Mares, in Spain; perhaps pertaining to the capricious behavior of an Arab mare. WM-3, DE-3

Hounds Earlier, protrusions on a wooden mast to support the trestletrees and the upper collars of some stays. (XV) On modern craft the same term applies to wooden and metal fittings by which the shrouds are secured. The term was used in Middle English, *hun*, and in Icelandic, *hunn*, then meaning the knob at the masthead. S-1, DE-4

House Flag The identifying flag of a company to which a merchant ship belongs; earlier, of her owner. (m. XVIII) To our best knowledge the custom of displaying this flag originated in the then-colonies, perhaps in Salem, Massachusetts. The Hanseatic League (XIII-XV) had its own flags, which, while not truly company flags, may well have been a beginning of this custom. S-3, T-1

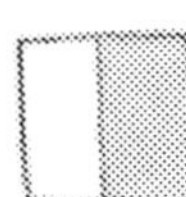

Housing Said of the part of the mast below the main deck, also of the inboard part of the bowsprit; sometimes called the bury. (XVII p.e.) The word probably comes, in this sense, from the Middle English *husing*, and the Old French *houce*, both of the same general meaning. (See *Bury*) DE-4

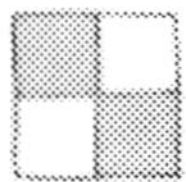

Hulk An old unseaworthy vessel, usually stripped of her gear, rigging, engines, etc. (XII) The word, seen in Middle English, Anglo-Saxon, and Latin, goes back to Greek, *elkas*, a type of ship. WS-1

Hull The body of any craft. (e. XV p.e.) The term comes from the Old English word *holhe*, meaning hollow. S-1, WS-1

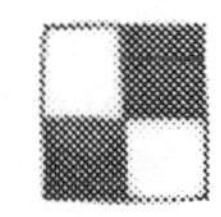

Hull Down Said of a vessel in the distance, when part or all of her hull is obscured from sight because of the curvature of the earth. (XVIII p.e.) F-1, DE-3

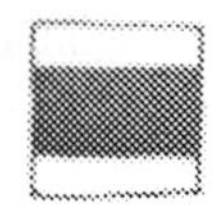

Idler Now called a dayman, a crew member who does not stand sea watches, such as various artificers and yeomen. (XVIII p.e.) The term was probably jocular, for the people who had "all night in." DE-3, JR

In (vs. On) a Ship Purists and our British cousins make a distinction here. "In" means to these being a member of a ship's company or of a yacht's crew, and "on" to being a passenger or a supernumerary. (XIX) JR

Inboard Said of anything inside the hull, outer rails, or outer rigging of a vessel. (p. XIV) (See *Aboard*) WO-1

Irish Hurricane A flat calm. Also called "Paddy's Gale." (XIX p.e.) K-1

Irish Pennant Any loose or unsecured line, or a frayed line or cloth. (XVIII p.e.) Originally a British term, it originated no doubt from the old and well-known low (and ill-deserved) regard by some Britons for people and things of Ireland. S-3

Irish Reef A method of shortening sail (sometimes in a hurry) on a gaff-rigged fore-and-after, by lowering the peak. (XVIII p.e.) (See *Scandalizing*) F-1b, S-3

Irons, In Said of a sailing craft when caught dead into the wind and unable without extra sail-handling to fill her sails on a new tack. (XVII p.e.) The term sometimes is used for a steamship that is badly trimmed or so lightly loaded that her propeller and rudder are ineffective. The origin of the term is uncertain; it could be from the sense of being in shackles, and unable to move. DE-3

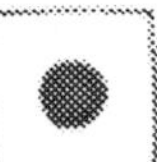

Ironsick An old term, still heard regarding old-fashioned wooden vessels with iron fittings or fastenings; of wood which is rotted due to chemical reaction from rusted iron. (e. XVII p.e.) The term appears to be sailors' or shipyard slang. DE-3

Isobar A line of equal barometric pressure on a weather map. (XIX) The word comes from the Greek, in tact, and means equal weight. DE-3

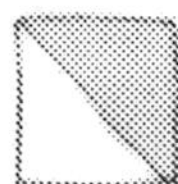

Isogonic Lines on a chart are the lines of equal magnetic variation. (XIX) The term comes from the Greek *isogon*, meaning equal angle. DE-3

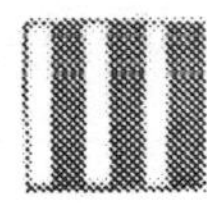

Jack (1) An adjective or prefix for a variety of gear and rigging, usually indicating that it is small or of a secondary purpose. (XVI p.e.) WW-1 (2) A small flag flown at the bow. (XVII p.e.) Of the U.S. jack, called the Union Jack, it is the union, or canon, of the ensign, and usually is displayed only when the ship is moored. WO-1 The derivation in both meanings is uncertain; it possibly is from Middle and Old French, *jacques*, among other things a colloquialism for small. DE-3

Jackass A plug for a hawsehole or hawspipe, to keep sea water out, or off the deck. (XIX p.e.) It probably was a sailor's nickname, possibly because some early ones looked like a small feed-bag. (See *Buckler*) D-3, DE-3

Jackrope An earlier term for the line securing a sail to a yard or spar, or to its jackstay. (XVII p.e.) (See *Earing, Jack, Lace Line*) F-1

Jackstay Earlier a rope, later a heavy rod, fastened to a square yard, to which a sail was bent. (l. XVIII) Also a line, later a rod or bar, in the crew quarters of a warship, for hanging hammocks, clothing, and other gear. F-1, S-3

Jacob's Ladder (1) Any ladder aloft except rattled shrouds. (XVII p.e.) The term was a sailor's nickname, and referred to the ladder by which the Biblical Jacob climbed to heaven. (See *Ratlines, Rattling Down*) (2) Also called a "Pilot's Ladder," a ladder that can be hung over the side of a ship for access to boats. (XVIII) Also too, a light ladder for shipside or for boat booms. (Both XVIII) WM-3, DE-4

Jamey Green (also *Jamie Green)* A quadrilateral fore-and-aft sail set under the bowsprit and jibboom by square-riggers when the wind was abeam. (XIX) This sail most often was used on the clipper ships, and is believed to have been named for a clipper's captain. M-4, S-3

Jeers A heavy tackle, usually made up with two triple blocks, for hoisting the yards on a square-rigger. (XV) An earlier spelling was jeares. The origin of the word is not known; it could be a corruption of shears. S-2, DE-4

Jetsam Anything thrown overboard to lighten ship; an earlier word was jetson. (XVI) The term comes from Anglo-Norman, *getteson*, and Old French, *getaison*, of the same meaning. WO-1

Jettison To throw cargo, stores, or gear overboard. The derivation is the same as for *jetsam*. WO-1

Jews' Harp A specially shaped shackle for yesteryear's stock anchors. The term is still used for an anchor shackle of any type. (e. XVII p.e.) It was named because it is shaped like an old fashioned jews' harp. DE-3

Jib Generally any fore-and-aft triangular sail on sailing craft of all sizes, and carried forward of the fore staysails on the larger ones. (XVII p.e.) Earlier the word was sometimes seen as gibb. The origin is obscure; it could be from Old Low German. A-2, WO-1

Jibboom (also *Jib Boom*) An extension of the bowsprit of a sailing vessel which, though fixed, is situated where the boom for a jib would be. A-2

Jibe A maneuver while sailing down wind, particularly in a fore-and-after, that shifts the sails from one side to the other. (XVII p.e.) The British spellings of this term are gibe, or gybe. The origin is Dutch, *gijbe*, of the same meaning. WS-1

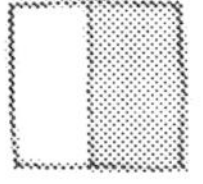

Jib-Headed (See *Bermuda, Marconi*)

Jib o' Jib(s) A large jib topsail rigged from the fore-royal stay of a square-rigger. (XIX) A light-weather sail, carried when on the wind, and mostly by packets and clippers. Simply, a super-jib. V-1

Jig A tackle at the end of any hauling line, as a halyard, used for several centuries to get that "extra foot" with a little help. (XVIII p.e.) The origin is obscure. DE-5

Jigger (1) The name of an after fore-and-aft sail, being different in location according to a vessel's rig; for example, a nickname for the mizzen on a modern yawl or ketch, and one of the after sails on the multi-masted schooner of yesteryear, according to the rigger's or the captain's fancy. (XIX) (2) Another name for jig, a tackle. (XVII) The origin of the term in both meanings is not certain. DE-3

Joggling The patterning of planking or plates in construction of a craft, usually for lapstrake boats. A joggling piece aids in this effort. (XVIII p.e.) The word probably comes from Celtic. B-6, DE-3

Jolly Roger The traditional decorative and identifying flag of pirates and buccaneers; usually black, with a design of macabre nature such as the well-known skull-and-crossed-bones. (XVIII) At that time rogues were called rogers. Jolly is a paradox, as they were anything but. Black was the traditional color, in the West Indies and the Mediterranean, of the renegade. WM-3

Jumbo Opinions vary on this term, but the prevailing one favors the large fore staysail of a Grand Banks fishing schooner; hence it refers to any fore staysail. (l. XIX) A good derivation is impossible, but it could be related to the ears of a large Barnum and Bailey elephant. DE-5, WAB, JR

Jumper (1) The stay from the tip of the jibboom to the lower end of the martingale boom, now usually of chain or wire rope. (XVIII) DE-3 (2) A short name for a jumper stay or strut, the former being a truss-like stay on the forward side of the mast of some craft. (XIX) DE-3 (3) A short pullover shirt or blouse worn by many sailors, formerly (and has come back as) part of a Navy sailor's uniform. DE-5

The origins for the first two meanings is not known; in the last it appears to be Middle English, *jupe*, a type of jacket.

Junk (1) Old rope. (p. XII) The term comes from *jonke*, a Middle English word of the same meaning. WO-1 (2) Any of several types of Chinese vessels, usually sail. The term is believed to come from a Portuguese-Mindinao word, *junce*—their name for this type of vessel. (XVI) Other sources were Javanese, *djong*, ship; and Malay, *adjong*, boat. (Both XVII p.e.) WO-1 (3) Salted beef served in the forecastle. (XVIII) The origin in this sense no doubt relates to junk (1). DE-4

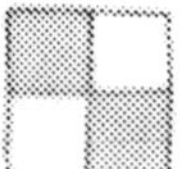

Jury A temporary or makeshift arrangement of any of a vessel's gear due to damage, such as a jury rudder. (XV) There are several possibilities for a derivation: one an Old French word, *jornal*, or *jurnal*, for the day, implying temporary; another, also Old French, *ajuirer*, to help, and this one goes back to Latin, *adiutare*, aid. S-1, WS-1

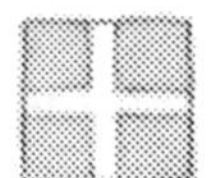

Keckling Old line wrapped or served around a hawser, especially the anchor cable, before the days of chain, to inhibit chafe. (e. XVII p.e.) The origin is not known; it could be from Dutch. M-2, DE-3

Kedge Earlier, to warp a ship or to move her by the use of an anchor; now only of the latter meaning. (XV) An earlier spelling was kadge. The word comes from Middle English, *caggen*, to catch or to fasten. (See *Warp*) S-2, WS-1, WO-1

Keel The "backbone" of a boat or ship; also on sailing craft the projecting structure extending below the bottom, for ballast and directional control. (XIII) This term goes back to the Old Norse word *kjolr*, ridge. It is one of many that is recognizable in other modern languages, in this case all the Teutonic. S-2, WO-1

Keel Hauling The cruel and usually lethal "punishment" of dragging a man from one side of a vessel to the other, under the keel. (e. XVII p.e.) The custom originated with the Dutch Navy, and the derivation, logically, is Dutch, *kielhalen*. It was phased out in the British and Dutch Navies in the early XVIII century. M-1, S-2

Keelson A reenforcing timber fastened inboard of and over the keel. It is sometimes seen as kelson, and often so pronounced. (XIII) *Kelson* was the Middle English; it probably came from Scandinavian. S-1, WO-1

Kenning An old term for the distance from which high land could be sighted at sea, about twenty miles. (XVI p.e.) The word comes from the Middle English *kennen*, make known. K-1, DE-3

Kentledge A type of inboard ballast. (XVII) This term comes from Old French, *quintelage*, of the same meaning. WO-1

Ketch Now a two-masted sailboat, the after mast (called the mizzen or jigger) being shorter, and generally stepped forward of the rudder post. An earlier definition was of a vessel with two masts, the relative sizes usually as in modern craft, but square-rigged. This craft was heavy, wide, and slow. (XV p.e.) The term probably came, via Middle English, from Old French, *quaiche*, of this latter definition. An earlier English term was *catche*. L-4, WAB

Kevel A large cleat or pair of bitts, in older sailing ships. Typical of older terms, there were several spellings, such as cavil, and chevil. (e. XVII p.e.) Its origin is Old French, *keville*, peg, or cleat. S-2, WS-1

Kid A small open barrel, also a large pan or pot. (e. XIX p.e.) The term came, via Middle English, from the Middle Dutch *kitte*, jug or tankard. As forecastle terms often are, this one is subject to corruption, such as the naval term spitkit, a seagoing cuspidor. WM-2, DE-4

Killick (also *Killeck*, etc.) Earlier a simple anchor, a rock or a weighted hook; later a grapnel type. It is also another word for sentinel, a weight on an anchor cable to improve the anchor's holding power. (XVII p.e.) The derivation is uncertain; it is possibly Old Norse. DE-3

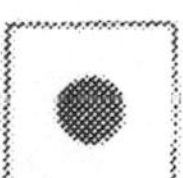

King Peg (See *King Spoke*)

King Post A short derrick mast on a merchant ship or a naval auxiliary. The term was referred to in the XVI century, but the nautical connotation is dubious. B-6, DE-3

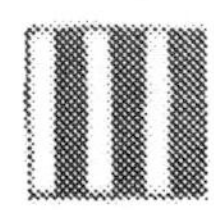

King Spoke (also *King Peg*) The spoke on a ship's wheel which, when upright, indicates that the rudder is amidships, or in line with the keel. (p. XVII) It very likely was so called because it often was identified and decorated with a crown or other regal emblem, honoring a monarch. Nowadays it is marked by a simple ornament, perhaps a turkshead or a metal cap. B-1, JR

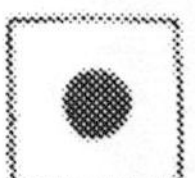

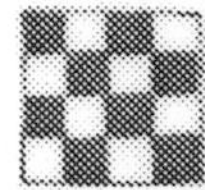

Kink An unwanted tight turn in a line. (e. XVII p.e.) The term appears to have several sources, the oldest of which is the Old Norse word ***kika***, bend. M-1, WS-1

Kippage Now a rare term for all the apparel and personnel of a vessel. (p. XV) Its origin is the Middle French *equipage*, one meaning of which was total equipment. DE-3

Ki-Yi A stiff-bristled brush for scrubbing a deck. (p. XIX) The term may well be a corruption of the word coir, as the bristles often were of coconut fiber. B-6

Knee An angular strengthening and supporting timber in a wooden craft, and the name for certain angular members in an iron or steel ship. (e. XVII p.e.) The term goes back to Old Saxon, ***knie***, knee, but when it took on a shipbuilding connotation is uncertain — it could have been XII or earlier. S-2, WO-1

Knightheads (1) Earlier (XVII p.e.) a pair of timbers serving as lateral bracing to the bowsprit of a wooden sailing ship. They also served as bitts and as a base for a windlass. (2) Later the knighthead became a bulwark or a bulkhead through which the bowsprit protruded. (XVIII) They are believed to be so-called as they often were carved in the form of a knight's helmet in earlier ships. (See ***Knights***). D-3, F-1, DE-3, WAB

Knights Now obsolete, knights were timbers in various locations on the deck of a sailing ship. Some were used to make lines fast and some had sheaves through which lines could be passed. (XV) There are several possibilities for the term's origin, the most likely being that they were often decorated with a carving, such as a knight's helmet. Another could have been the Old English *cnotta*, knot. On some older ships there were twelve, and sometimes were called apostles, which see. S-2, M-1, WO-1, WAB

Knittle (See *Nettle*)

Knockabout A fishing schooner and pleasure boat rig which has no bowsprit, or had only a very short one in the days when a long one was customary. (1.XIX) The first Grand Banks schooner so rigged was built in 1902. For pleasure craft the rig originated in Marblehead, Mass., in 1892. The term probably came into being as a colloquialism; the typical knockabout was characterized as being husky. C-1b, DE-5, WAB

Knock Off is to stop work or whatever one is doing. A standard order possibly well before the XVIII century, it comes from the days when galleys were rowed to the rhythm of mallets on a block, and the signal to rest was so given. (XV p.e.) DE-3

Knot A long story could be written on this term. (1) A general term for tying a rope to an object, or, improperly, to another rope. (XIV) (See *Bend*) It has several sources: Anglo-Saxon *knotta*, Old Norse *knuta*, and Old English *cnotta*, all meaning knot. S-1 (2) A vessel's rate of speed, a nautical mile per hour. (e. XVII p.e.) Briefly, this was attained by running-out astern a line that was knotted at measured intervals, and timing the run with a timeglass. (See *Chip Log, Log*) This is a term that is recognizable in all of the modern Teutonic languages. WO-1

Knuckle An edge or a ridge formed by the change in form of the hull, such as of the flare forward, or the shaping of the upper works of the stern. (p. XVIII) It is a shipbuilder's term, and probably came from early Dutch. DE-5, DVR

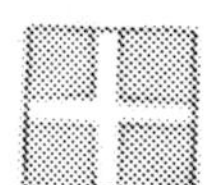

Kort Nozzle A short, molded cylindrical fitting built around the propeller of a vessel requiring good maneuverability, to increase its thrust. (e. XX) It was named for its inventor, a German engineer. M-1

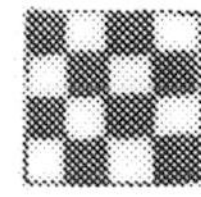

Lace Line (also *Lacing*) A line used to secure a sail to its yard or spars. (XIII) The word in this sense is from the Middle English *lass*, lash or tie, probably from Old French, *laz*, tie. M-2, DE-3

Ladder On shipboard, not only a ladder *per se*, but all stairs too, except perhaps on passenger ships. (XIV) They were always called that probably because they usually were steep and narrow, and nearly always removable, as they are now. The origin of the word is Anglo-Saxon, *hlaeder*, of the same meaning. S-2, DE-3

Lagan Any heavy article thrown overboard and buoyed, for possible recovery. (XVIII p.e.) The term comes from the Anglo-French word of the same spelling and possibly of the same meaning. WS-1

Landfall The sighting of land from at sea (sometimes a very happy event). (e. XVII p.e.) The derivation of fall in this context is obscure. S-2, DE-3

Landlubber A shoresider, especially one who knows little about the water. (XVI) Lubber comes from Anglo-Saxon, also from old French. (See ***Lubber***) DE-3, WW-1

Lanyard (1) Any light line to make an object fast or to aid in carrying it. (2) The line by which a sailing ship's shroud is secured to a chainplate; still used in traditional rigging in yachts. (Both e. XVII p.e.) Earlier the word was lannier; its origin was Old French, *larniére*, earlier *lasniére*, thong or noose. S-2, WO-1

Lapstrake The planking of a craft of which the lower edge of each strake overlaps that below it; a very old and a worldwide technique. The word comes from Old Saxon, *lepel*, overlap. (See ***Clinker, Strake***) B-8, DE-4

Larboard The old word for the port side of any craft. (e. XVII p.e.) My sources indicate that the term went back to the XII or XIII century in English; the Middle English word was *laddebord*, for loading side. In the days of the side rudder, or steering oar, it was nearly always on the starboard side, so a vessel tied port, or larboard side, to the shore, to protect the rudder from possible damage. The term goes back to all the nordic languages; the Old Norse word was *hlada bord*, meaning loading side. (See *Port*) S-2, WO-1, WAB

Large An old term for sailing free, or before the wind. (XIV) It possibly comes from the Latin *largus*, abundant. Its nautical connection is obscure. M-2, WW-1

Lash To tie something securely. (XVI) The term comes from Middle English, *lasche*, to tie, and possibly from Old French. (See *Lace Line*) S-2, WO-1

Lateen A triangular fore-and-aft sail on a long yard, at deck level forward and high aft, and loosefooted. The term applies to both the sail and the rig. (e. XVIII p.e.) It is believed to have been named by both British and French sailors, and the word to be a corruption of the word Latin in both languages. This type of sail and rig have been in use in the Mediterranean from about the IX century. WS-1, DE-3

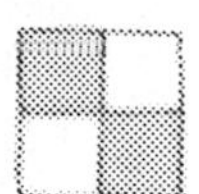

Launch (1) A ship's boat, also a personnel boat. (XVII p.e.) The word in this sense comes from the Spanish *lancha*, a pinnace, and could come from Malaysian. WO-1
(2) To put a ship or boat into the water. (XIV) In this sense the term came from the Anglo-Saxon *launcher*, of this meaning, and could go back to Latin. WO-1

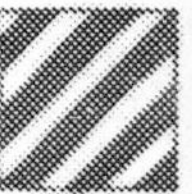

Lay (1) A noun, describing the twist in the strands of cordage. (2) A verb, of several meanings: one, an order, as to lay aloft, or lay aft—to go there; another, said of a vessel sailing on the wind, if she can lay an objective, or reach it without tacking. (Both e. XVII p.e.) The term came from Old English, *laegen*, of the same meanings. S-2, DE-3

Lazarette A small hold or locker, usually in the stern, for stores and gear. (XVIII p.e.) The term apparently came from the Italian word *lazaretto*, which meant an isolation hospital, which often was in a ship or hulk. The connection is obscure, but it could be that the ward of such a vessel often was in the after section, as was the sickbay in the bigger warships. S-3, DE-3

Lazy A general term for any line or gear that does not move or is not often in use. (e. XVIII) The origin of the term probably is either from Low German, *lasich*, or Dutch, *leuzig*, both implying waiting. WS-1

Lazy Jacks Lines rigged from high on a mast to the boom on a fore-and-after, to facilitate dropping or scandalizing a sail quickly. (XVIII) It is probable that this device was invented by Hudson River sailors, whose sailing cargo boats were occasionally hit by squalls and sudden shifts of wind. L-4

Leach (See *Leech*)

Lead, The A molded piece of lead with a line attached, for sounding, i.e., for measuring the water's depth and testing the bottom. (XVI) The origin of the term in its maritime meaning is not known; but the lead or its equivalent was surely the first navigational equipment. Its use has been documented in 2060 B.C. B-1, K-1

League An old measure of distance of three nautical miles. (XVI p.e.) The term comes from the Latin *leuga*, a Gallic mile, and is still used in Scandinavian languages. WS-1, DE-3

Lee Away from the directional force of the wind. (XIV) The origin is probably Old Saxon, *lee*, or Old Norse, *hle*, possibly both, and both of this meaning. WO-1, WS-2

Leeboards Drop-keels on the side of some sailing vessels, especially those of the Low Countries, where they originated. (XV) They are also seen in North America on lake sailboats and canoes. They were in common use on the Hudson River and on Chesapeake Bay into the early XX. K-1, WS-1, WAB

Leech The trailing or after edge of a fore-and-aft sail, also an outer edge of a square sail.(XIV) The word appears to come from late Middle English, *leche*. S-1, WS-1

Leechline (also *Leech Line*) A line for "spilling" or furling a square sail. (e. XVII p.e.) S-2, WS-1

Leeward In a position or direction away from that of the wind. (XIV) One scholar writes that an old spelling was lewward, which appears to account for the mariner's pronunciation of "looward." S-2, WS-1

Leg-o'-Mutton A triangular sail, a forerunner of the *Marconi* or *Bermuda*. (m. XVII) The origin is uncertain; it appears to be a nickname relating to its resemblance to the product. DE-4, WAB

Letter of Marque A royal license, authorizing a vessel to privateer under a recognized flag. (l. XIII) *Marque* is Old French, in this sense meaning to seize as a pledge; it came from Late Latin, *marcare*, of the same meaning. K-1, WS-1

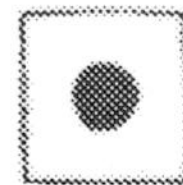

Lewis Bolt An eyebolt in a vessel's deck, socketed and wedged under the deck for extra strength. (XVIII) Its origin is believed to be a proper name, no doubt for the conceiver. M-1, WO-1

Liberty A seaman's short shore leave. This is now considered to be a navy man's term, but appears to go back to apply to all seamen since ca. XV. N-4, DE-5

Lifts Lines to support and control the 'thwartship, or lateral angle of a square-rigger's yard. (XVII) The word comes from Middle English, *lifte*, of this sense. S-2, WO-1

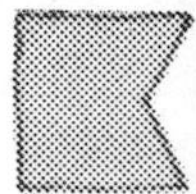

Limbers Holes in the frames close to the keel or keelson, to allow for restricted flow of bilge water. (e. XVII p.e.) The word is believed to come from the Old French *lumiere*, one meaning of which was hole. (Of light, there was little!) S-2, WO-1

Limejuicer (also *Limey*) Our nickname, in sailing-ship days and now, for a British ship and her people. (XVIII) Limes and limejuice had been discovered to be a preventative for a common shipboard disease, scurvy; they became a required ration first in British ships, for this purpose. K-1, JR

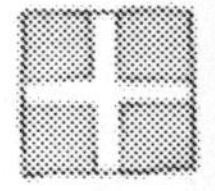

Line As we all know, almost every piece of rope of any craft that has a designated use is called a line, and the word's origin may tell you why. (XV) The word comes from the Latin *linea*, thence Old French *ligne*, then Old English, *line*, and Middle English, *ligne*; all mean rope. (See *Rope*) WO-1

Liner Now the almost obsolete passenger ship that makes a scheduled run on a regular route, operated by a steamship line or company. It was the earlier nickname in the British Navy for a ship of the line, a major warship. (XVIII) K-1, T-1

Lines The diagrammatic drawings of the design of a ship's hull. (e. XIX p.e.) The word comes from the Middle English *linen*, a ship's lines or appearance. Space prohibits a story on this, but suffice it to say that ship design from the drawing board became a recognized technique during the XVIII century. Plans for component parts of a ship were seen in the early XV, and for hull forms in the late XV. P-2, S-3, WAB

List Both a noun and a verb, referring to a vessel's tipping due to improper trim, cargo shiifting, a heavy wind, etc. (XIII) The word no doubt comes from the Anglo-Saxon *lystan*, to lean. S-1, WO-1

Listless Is another sea term that came ashore (XVII) It meant having no wind, hence no list, ergo lifeless. N-5

Lizard A lanyard fitted with a block or a bull's eye at one end, as a fairlead. (e. XVII p.e.) The derivation is not known. DE-3

Loaded Originally a sailor's term for being drunk —"loaded to the marks" or "to the gills." (XVIII p.e.) WM-3

Load Line (See *Plimsoll Mark*)

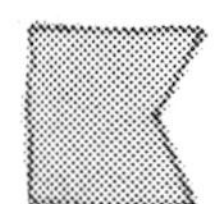

Loblolly Boy A surgeon's assistant aboard ship in the XVI to XVIII centuries. Loblolly was the name for the gruel or porridge usually served to the surgeon's customer in the sickbay. K-12, DE-5

Lobscouse (also *Scouse*) A hash served in the crew's quarters. (p. XVII) The origin of the word is uncertain. It is very probably from the German *lobskaus*, a praiseworthy dish (which it wasn't). DE-3

Lock A chamber with gates, on a canal made up of sections of different levels of water, by which a vessel can be raised or lowered to float in the succeeding section. (XVI) The term comes from the Old English word, *loc*, meaning barrier. WO-1

Locker A shipboard cabinet, cupboard or small store or workroom. (e. XVII p.e.) Its origin is the same as for lock, in this sense meaning to lock. M-2

Log (1) The name of a device that measures speed or distance travelled through the water. (XVI) An early method of estimating speed was simply to throw a log (or a large piece of wood) over the side at the bow and to measure the time it took for the object to pass a point at the stern. Hence the name. (See *Chip Log, Knot*) (2) Also called the logbook, the document (required on all commercial and government vessels) recording all navigational data and all the major events and activities of the vessel and her people. (p. XVII) It no doubt got its name as being the record of data from *Log* (1). To make an entry in this record is known as logging.

The word appears to have Teutonic derivation, but to have had an earlier English origin. S-2, DE-3

Loggerhead (1) Earlier called loggerheat, a ball or knob of iron on a long staff, used when heated to melt pitch or tar for caulking and other repairs. Also a wicked weapon. (XVI) (2) The single large bit in the stern of a whaleboat, used to control the harpoon line when ''fast'' to a whale. (XVIII) (3) A name for bar-shot fired by some ship's guns. (p. XVI)

The origin of the term in the three senses is obscure. F-1, WW-1

Long Stay An old term for a long anchor rode, usually four or more times the depth of water. (XVIII p.e.) The use of the word stay in reference to anchoring is obscure in origin, but it appears to have the meaning of to hold, rather than referring to a ship's rigging. DE-5

Loof An old term, still heard, for the tapering (sic) of the hull toward the bow and the stern. (e. XIII) The derivation of the term is probably Icelandic, *loffi*, possibly of the same meaning. (See *Luff*) S-1, DE-4

Loom (1) The shaft of an oar. (XVII p.e.) The origin is uncertain; it may be from the Middle English *lome*, tool or part of one. WP-1c (2) An atmospheric effect; for example from shore lights from at sea, or the "rosy fingers of the dawn." (XVIII) The word in this sense comes from Anglo-Saxon, *leoma*, ray of light. WW-1

Loran An international electronic system for off-shore navigation, to fix a ship's position. (m. XX) The word is an acronym, adapted first by the U.S. and British navies during World War II—LOng RAnge Navigation. N-4

Lubber An awkward or not-too-bright sailor or workman. (XVI p.e.) The origin is Anglo-Saxon, *lobbe*, a slow, clumsy person. WO-1

Lubber's Hole A hole in a square rigger's top next to the mast through which the heads of the shrouds pass to the mast. (p. XVIII) It is so named as a passage aloft for a lubber, the real sailor going "out and around" on the futtock shrouds. (See *Futtock Shrouds, Tops, The*) K-1

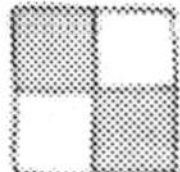

Lubber's Lines Marks in the bowl of a ship's compass, aligned for dead ahead, astern, and abeam. (XIX p.e.) The origin of the term may be that an experienced helmsman did not need these aids to ascertain the ship's heading, and to use them was considered lubberly. Pub-2

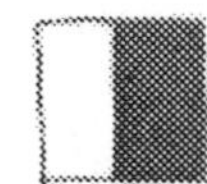

Lucky Bag Mostly a naval colloquialism, the lost-and-found department. (XIX p.e.) This is a good example of sailors' whimsy, as to recover a lost article could cost a man a fine, and earlier a piece of rope's end served him uncomfortably. L-8, N-4

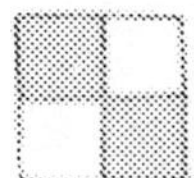

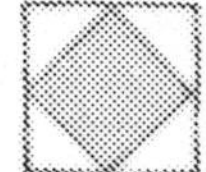

Luff is a term with a variety of definitions over the years. (1) An old one, rare now, is the area forward on a vessel where the rails or bulwarks begin to converge toward the bow; earlier, loof. (XIII) WS-1 (2) The forward or leading edge of a fore-and-aft sail. (e. XVII p.e.) WO-1 The origin in this meaning is obscure, but could refer to the following: (3) A verb to turn a sailing craft into the wind and so spill the wind from her sails. (e. XVII p.e.) Here again the origin is uncertain; it could come from an earlier definition, a paddle or oar used forward to assist in turning. WS-1 (4) To raise the outer end of a cargo boom or crane. (XIX p.e.) This may be a salty corruption of lift. JR

Lug A sail and a rig of several types for small craft. (XVII p.e.) The word is probably Old English in origin, borrowed by the Dutch with their word *logger*, and taken back again into English. WS-1

Lugger (1) A lug-rigged craft. (XVIII p.e.) (2) A general term for a small work-a-day vessel, either harbor or coastal. (XVIII) (See *Lug*) WO-1

Lutine Bell A bell mounted at Lloyd's headquarters in London, rung as notice of an important announcement. It was the ship's bell of H.M.S. *Lutine*, which sank off the Dutch coast in a storm in 1799. K-1

Luting A mixture used on connecting surfaces of timbers in building and repairing wooden craft, a bedding compound. (XIV) The word goes back, via Old French, to Latin, *lutum*, a type of clay. D-3, WO-1

Lyle Gun A small cannon for firing a "dead" projectile to which a strong light line is attached; used for rescue purposes. (l. XIX) It is named for its inventor David A. Lyle, an officer in the coast artillery. DE-5

McNamara's Lace A navy slang term, sometimes heard in merchant ships, for the almost-disappeared "fancy work," such as macrame curtains, cushions, and ornaments. (p.m. XIX) It is said to have been named for an old boatswain, but another possibility is that it is a corruption of macrame. N-4

Macrame More often called "fancy work" by seamen, the term covers knotting and braiding of a large variety of basic and ornamental articles. The term appeared in the XIX century, but the art is an old one. The origin could be Turkish, *makrame*, towel, or Arabic, *megrama*, striped cloth. WO-1

Magazine The special hold, existing earlier in virtually all ocean-going ships, and now in naval vessels, in which ammunition is stowed. (XVII p.e.) The direct derivation is Old French, *magazin*, storehouse or storeroom, which appears to come from the Arabic *makhazin*, storehouse. DE-3

Maiden Voyage The first voyage of a vessel. (XVIII p.e.) The word comes from the sense of "new," or "first time," and of course relates to the custom that all ships and boats are "she's." DE-3

Main applies to many things on almost any sized craft, such as mainmast, mainsail, main engines, main hatch, etc., and implies size or importance. (XV p.e.) The word's derivation is Latin, *magnus*, great; it was seen in Old Norse, *mageus*, Old English, *maegen*, and Old French, *maine*, all meaning basically the same thing. A-2, WO-1

Make has several meanings at sea: (1) To arrive at a desired point. (XVI) (2) To attain a certain speed. (XVII p.e.) (3) To accomplish an act, as to make sail. (XIV) The word's origin in these senses appears to be the same as for others: *make* in Middle English and the Old English *macian*, to do. DE-3

Make Fast To fasten a line, especially to a cleat or to bitts. (XIII) Fast is from the same word in Anglo-Saxon. (See *Fast*) S-2, DE-3

Make Water To take in water from a leak or hull damage. (XIV) The term is a translation of a French term for the same unhappy phenomenon, *faire d'eau*. DE-3

Man As a the verb, to put the necessary number of men to a function, such as the capstan, boat falls, etc., also to furnish a ship with a crew. (e. XVII p.e.) The word in this sense comes from Old English, same word and meaning. M-2, DE-3

Manger Now a foredeck breakwater; earlier it had the same function but below. It was abaft the hawseholes, which were on a lower deck. (e. XVII p.e.) The origin of the word in its nautical meaning is obscure; it appears to have come from Middle English, and from the French *mangeoire*, manger, farm style. S-2, DE-4

Manhelper A long pole to which a paintbrush or scraper can be attached, for working on a ship's side or bottom when in drydock. (XVIII p.e.) The term appears to be a down-easter's nickname. JR

Manifest A master document of a merchant ship for regulatory purposes: a listing of her cargo, passengers, etc., with appropriate details. (XVIII p.e.) The word came, via Old French, *manifester*, from the Latin *manifestare*, declaration. WO-1

Manila Cordage made from the leaf fibers of the Abaca plant, which is native to the Philippines. It is stronger and more durable than other hemp cordage. (XVIII) WO-1

Manropes Lines hung over the side in various ways, to facilitate ascent or descent on a side ladder; usually ornamented. (e. XVII p.e.) M-2, DE-5

Marconi (1) The early name for "CW" (continuous wave) radio, its equipment and techniques. (e. XX) It got its name, lest we forget, from Guglielmo Marconi, the Nobel Prize-winning inventor. DE-1 (2) The modern sailboat rig and its major sails. The term first applied to the vast array of standing rigging of the great gaff-rigged racing cutters, and no doubt related to their similarity to a radio antenna mast. (e. XX) The term has since become associated with the *Bermuda* rig, first seen in the U.S. on Long Island Sound in 1895. The Star class, the oldest international one-design racing sailboat class, adopted the rig in 1922. It reached the America's Cup competition in the J boats of 1930. (See *Bermuda*) R-2, WAB

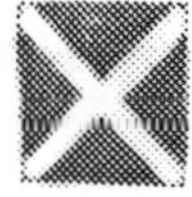

Marina A harbor, usually at least partially man-made and for small craft. (XIX p.e.) The word came from either Italian or Spanish, possibly both, and thence from Latin, *marinus*, harbor. DE-4

Marine (1) Almost anything to do with the water. (XV) The word comes from Latin, *mare*, the sea, via Old French and Anglo-Norse. WO-1 (2) The well-known "Soldier of the Sea." The U.S. Marine Corps was founded in 1775. N-4

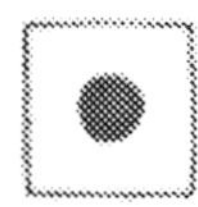

Maritime The term has much the same meanings as marine. (XV) The word probably comes from Old French, and goes back to the Latin *maritimus*, near to or of the sea. WO-1

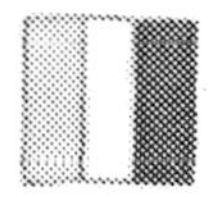

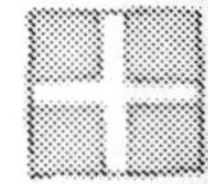

Mark (1) A guiding device to the mariner, such as a beacon or a buoy. (XV) K-2 (2) A depth indicator on a lead-line. (XVIII p.e.) The marking of sounding lines for depth is almost ageless—it is only the term that is relatively new. DE-5 (See *Lead, The*) (3) An order, such as to an assistant of the navigator, to note the exact time on a sextant sight, or to report that the ship is exactly on course, etc. (XVII p.e.) The origin of the term in these meanings is difficult to trace. It has French connections, but more likely it is Nordic and from the Old English *mearcen*, mark. DE-3

Marl To tie or serve a line with a series of hitches, such as a marling hitch or a half hitch. (XV) The term came from Middle Dutch, *merren*, to tie. (See *Marline*) WO-1

Marline (also *Marlin*) Two-stranded small stuff, treated with pine-tar as a preservative, of a myriad of uses. (XV) An earlier spelling was marling. There is a difference of opinion on the word: one that is from Dutch, *marlijn*, binding line, and another from Middle English, *marlyne*, this from Old English. Both could be right. WO-1

Marline Spike A tapered and pointed metal tool, used in rope working, especially for splicing. (e. XVII p.e.) Earlier it was known as a marling spike. DE-3

Martinets (also *Martnets*) An arrangement of lines, now obsolete, for brailing square sails. (XV) The derivation is obscure; it probably was Middle English. S-2, DE-3

Martingale (1) A stay running from the forward end of a jibboom or spike bowsprit of a sailing vessel, to the end of a strut under the bowsprit called a martingale boom, also dolphin striker. (XVIII) (2) The spar itself is sometimes called a martingale. The term was adopted from the horse world, in which it is a strap to hold a horse's head from moving up excessively. It came from Middle English. A-2, WO-1

Maru The word after the name of virtually every Japanese craft, large or small, except for their naval vessels. It is said to be symbolic of perfection or completeness. M-1

Mast A principal vertical spar. (XV p.e.) The origin of the term appears to be two-fold: Old Norse, *mastr*, and Anglo-Saxon, *maest*. The traditional names of the three masts seen from the XVI century, the fore, main, and mizzen, go back to at least the XVII. S-1, WO-1

Master The legal title for the captain of a merchant ship. Until the mid or late XIX, a master was not in command; he was in effect a warrant officer in charge of the actual sailing of the vessel, but not of what she was to accomplish. The word goes back, via Old English and Anglo-Saxon, to Latin, *magistrum*, meaning master. A master mariner is a merchant marine officer who is licensed and qualified for command. S-2, WO-1

Mate (1) A deck officer below the rank of captain in a merchant ship. (Many have masters' licenses.) (2) One of a number of petty officers' ratings in the services. The word came, via Middle English, from earlier Dutch, *maet*, mate or assistant. S-2,WO-1

Matthew Walker A type of stopper knot. (e. XIX) This is said to be the only knot named for its inventor, who is believed to have been a rigger in a British navy yard. A-3a

Mayday The distress call for voice radio, for vessels and people in serious trouble at sea. The term was made official by an international telecommunications conference in 1948, and is an anglicizing of the French *m'aidez*, "help me." N-4, JR

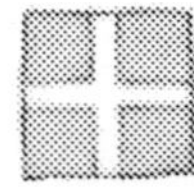

Mercator A conformed projection type of chart used extensively in navigation. (XVI) It was named for its conceiver, Gerardus Mercator, the Latinized name of Gerhard Kramer, a noted Flemish scientist. DE-1

Mess (1) A group within a ship's company who live and eat together, such as the junior officers' mess. (2) A shipboard meal, or food in general. (p. XVI) The word came from Middle English, *mes*, and goes back to Late Latin, *missum*, that which is put on the table. It is a military as well as a seafarer's term. WW-1

Messenger A light line, bent to a heavier one, such as a heaving line for a mooring hawser. Also, the endless line passed round the capstan and through blocks on deck to provide the motive force in weighing anchor in larger, old sailing ships. (See *Nipper*) (m. XVIII, almost certainly much earlier) Found in Middle English, not for certain in the nautical sense, the word comes from Old French, *messagier*, forerunner. S-3, DE-5

Midshipman (1) Earlier, a boy in his early teens who went to sea to learn to be an officer, both in the navy and the merchant service (more a British and European custom than an American one). (e. XVII) (2) The title given to student officers at our Naval Academy and in N.R.O.T.C. programs. (XIX) The term came about as earlier these young men usually were quartered amidships, forward of the officers and abaft the crew. WO-1, JR

Misstay The act of failing to complete the process of tacking or coming about. Earlier the term was spelled out, miss stays. (XVIII p.e.) (See *Stays*) DE-3

Mitch Board An earlier term for a boom crutch, also a rack for stowing extra spars. (p. XVI) This is a rare one in the U.S., but I am told it still is used sometimes in Britain. The word comes from Middle Dutch, *micke*, forked stick, and may go back to Viking days. DE-3

Mitten Money Extra pilotage fee charged a vessel in very cold weather. (p. XVIII) The word mitten comes from Old French. D-3

Mizzen The aftermost mast and its sails and gear, on a two- or three-masted vessel: generally the third mast aft on a vessel with more than three masts (the exception being brigs and two-masted schooners, the after masts of which are called main rather than mizzen). (XV) Earlier it was spelled mizen. The term comes from the Middle English *mesan*, goes back to Italian *mazzane*, Late Latin *medianus*, middle or mid-size, and apparently is of Arabic origin, *misan*, balance. It did and does serve as a balancing sail. S-1, WO-1

Monkey Generally, any small or light gear or structure, such as a monkey chain, monkey bridge, gaff, or rail. It appears to have been a XIX century slang term for anything diminutive. S-3, DE-3

Monkey Jacket The nickname given to several items of mariner's apparel, such as the short jackets worn in the early days of uniforms for enlisted men, later for midshipmen, and also for the mess jacket still worn by navy and merchant marine officers. It undoubtedly got its name from its similarity to the jackets worn by circus and carnival monkeys. WM-3

Monkey's Blood The British Navy wardroom nickname for red wine. (p. XVII) R.N.

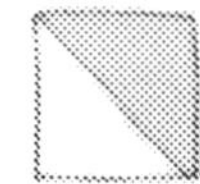

Moonraker The highest sail on a square-rigger's mast, in the days of the clipper ships. (XIX) DE-3

Moor Briefly, the act of fastening a ship or boat to the shore or to the bottom. (e. XVII p.e.) The term came from Middle English, *more*, thence from Old English, *maerels*, both of the same general meaning; also from Dutch, *marren*, to tie or fasten. M-2, WS-1

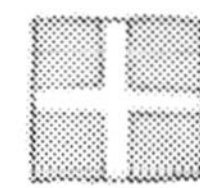

Morse Code The international "CW" (continuous wave) radio code. (e. XX) It got its name from Samuel F.B. Morse, the famed inventor of the telegraph, who developed the first code for its use. DE-4

Mother Carey's Chickens A sailor's name for stormy petrels. (XVIII p.e.) The name is believed to be a corruption of the Latin *mater cara*, tender mother, referring to the Virgin Mary. Sailors believed that these little sea birds were under her special care, due to their hardiness, beauty, size, and skill in flight. (If you have ever seen them "in weather" at sea, you probably are a believer.) DE-3, Pub-2

Mouse To enclose a hook or hank with small stuff. (XVIII p.e.) Earlier, a mousing was a bulky knotting on a stay; it was pear, or mouse shaped. The evolution of the term to its present sense is obscure. DE-3

Napier Card *(also Napier Diagram)* A diagram giving compass bearings on various headings of a ship, for converting "magnetic" to "compass" and vice versa. (e. XVII) This very useful device was developed by Lord John Napier, a Scottish mathematician. M-1, S-3

Nautical The general word pertaining to ships and the sea. (XVI) It came from the Latin *nauticus*, and that from the Greek *nautikos*, both of this same meaning. WO-1

Naval Any thing or person related to a navy. (XVI) The word comes from the Latin *navalis*, loosely pertaining to ships, and could come from the Greek *naus*, ship. (See *Navy*) WO-1

Navigation The broad term for the management of a ship's or boat's movements. (XV p.e.) The term comes, via French, from the Latin *navigatere*, navigate. WO-1

Navy Navies as we know them today are a fairly recent development. The first known "navy" was Assyrian, ca. 700 B.C., a fleet of ships with armed men aboard. Later the term meant any gathering of ships, not necessarily armed (XIV); and yet later it meant that they were armed (XVI). Modern navies could be said to have been in the early stages of development in the late XVII and early XVIII centuries. The derivation of the word is a bit vague, but it did come from Old French, *navie*, fleet, and goes back to the Latin *navalis*, as for naval. WO-1

Neap Tide An extremely low tide. (XIV) While this book has only a few terms of natural phenomena, this one is included not only because of the importance of tides to the mariner, but especially because of one version of its origin: Old English *nep*, aground. WO-1

Near To sail too close to the wind; to "pinch." (XV) The order to the helmsman, "no near" meant no higher. S-2, DE-3

Nettle A short line or sennit for lashing a small object. (XVII) An earlier word was knittle, of which nettle appears to be a corruption, and which comes from the Old English *cynttan*, knitting. S-2, DE-3

Nibbling (also *Nibbing*) refers to the pointed shapes of the ends of certain deck planks, to fit either the kingplank or the covering boards. (p. XV; surely XVII) The word comes from the Anglo-Saxon *nebb*, beak. DE-3

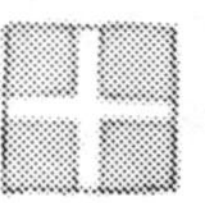

Niggerhead (1) Another term for gipsy head, on a winch or windlass. (XVIII) (See *Gipsy*) (2) A large single bollard on shoreside. (XVIII) This is a nickname in both senses, now rarely used. DE-3

Nip (1) A loop of an eye splice, or of a line spliced around a thimble or grommet. (XIV) (2) A kink or turn in a line. (XIV) (3) Said of a line when it breaks in direction, as in a block or chock. (e. XVII p.e.) (See *Freshen*) (4) (See *Nipper*) (5) A short snort. (p. XVI) The origin in the first four senses is not known; in the fifth it is Dutch, *nippen*, meaning the same thing. M-2, WW-1

Nipper (1) In the days of manhandling a large heavy anchor cable that was too large to go around a capstan, short lines called nippers were temporarily bound around the incoming cable and the continuously moving messenger, allowing the messenger to haul the cable aboard. (See *Messenger*) M-2 (2) A deck boy who lashed and freed the nipper to and from the cable; hence the old slang word, nipper, for deck boy. (See *Nip*) K-1 (3) A device for controlling the amount of tarring of rope standing rigging. (XVIII p.e.) The origin of the term in this sense is uncertain; it possibly is early Dutch. DE-3

Nock Another name for the throat of a gaff sail. (XVIII) Earlier, the end of a yard. (XVI) The term's origin is uncertain; it appears to be, via Middle English, early Dutch, *nokke*, meaning tip. DE-3, S-2

Noggin A tub, usually made from an old keg or cask; also a drinking mug. (p. XVII) The word probably came from Gaelic. M-1, WO-1

No Man's Land The area in the waist of a ship that is vulnerable to shipping seas in rough weather and is often cluttered with gear and stores. (XVIII) The name seems to speak for itself. F-1, V-1a

Norman (1) A pin to lock a capstan, to belay it and the cable temporarily. (2) A crossbar on bitts. (3) A pin or stud to lock a rudder in a given position. (All XVIII p.e.) It may be a corruption of normal, in the sense of a right angle, which came from the Latin *normalis*, made square. DE-3

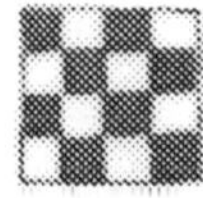

North Sea Organ The nickname for a concertina or an accordion. (XIX) These were popular instruments, especially in Scandinavian and German ships, to enjoy in good weather, or by the "watch below." NMMG, JR, KK

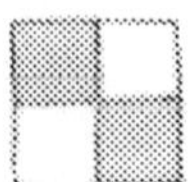

Norwegian Piano A nickname for the foghorn on a sailing ship. (l. XIX) It is a familiar sound in Northern European waters. JR, KK

Norwegian Steam A nickname for the sailor's equivalent of "elbow grease," handling any heavy gear with no machinery or little mechanical advantage. (p. XIX) JR, KK

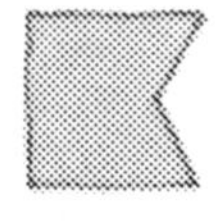

Nun Buoy A buoy that is conically shaped in its visible portion. (e. XVII p.e.) It appears to have gotten its name from the early English word *nun*, for a child's top that was tapered on both ends. The word comes from Old English, *nunna*, of the latter meanings. M-2, DE-3

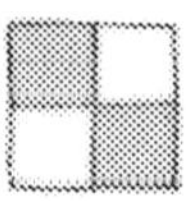

Nuts The protrusions on the shank of an anchor to keep the stock in place. (e. XVII p.e.) The word comes from Old English, but it is not known when it came to have this particular meaning. S-2, DE-3

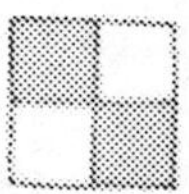

Nylon A synthetic fiber from which sails and cordage are made; renowned for its many good qualities. (XX) At first a trade name by its maker, DuPont, it has become a general term. B-6

Oakum Caulking material made of tarred yarn fibers, earlier of flax, the latter also called tow. (XV p.e.) The origin of the word is Anglo-Saxon, *acumba*, tow; the Middle English sometimes was *ockam*. M-2, WS-1

Oar An implement for rowing and sometimes steering a boat. (XV p.e.) The word goes back to Viking days, Old Norse (also Anglo-Saxon) *ar*; Middle English was *ore*. WO-1

Oarlock Any of several types of fulcrum for an oar. (p. XV) It comes from the Middle English *orlock*, and no doubt goes farther back. WO-1

Ocean The total sea mass (XIII), or the same in regions (XIV). The term goes the route; via Middle English, the same word; Old English and Old French, *occean*; Latin, *oceanus*; and Greek, *okeanos*. WO-1

Octant (1) An instrument for measuring altitude angles of celestial bodies. (m. XVII) (2) A rudder yoke in the shape of an arc of 45°. (XIX) The word is made up from Latin, *octo*, eight, and *angulus*, angle WS-1

Officer hardly needs definition. (XVI in the mariner's sense.) The word comes from Old French, *official*, and goes back to the Late Latin *officiarius*, for officer or leader. WO-1

Offing Being in sight of land but having adequate sea room. (e. XVII p.e.) It is possibly a sailor's coined word, for being off from the shore. M-2, WS-1

Oil Used for many purposes long before it became a ship's principal fuel; for lamps, to waterproof clothing, to "pour on troubled waters," and to preserve decks and rigging. (p. XII) The Middle English word was *oile*; it goes back to Latin, *oleum*, from *olea* and to Greek, *elaia*, both for olive tree. WS-1

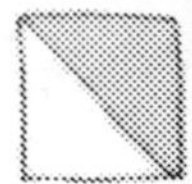

Oilskins Earlier called oil cloth, garments treated with linseed or other oils for waterproofing (XVII p.e.) DE-3

Omni The better-known short word for omnirange, a radio navigation system. (m. XX) Omni comes from the Latin *omnis*, all. DE-4

Orlop The lowest full-length deck of an early sailing ship, the word is still heard on some modern merchant vessels. (XV) Earlier it was a partial deck, especially of smaller ships. The word appears to come from this latter meaning, and is from the Dutch, *overlope*, overlap, via Middle English. S-1, WS-1

O.S. Ordinary seaman, a rating in the merchant marine below that of "A.B." (XVII p.e.) It was formally established in the U.S. merchant marine in 1915. DE-3

Outboard Anything outside the rails, sides, or ends of any craft. (XIV) Out in this sense comes from the Anglo-Saxon *ute*, out from. (See *Board*) S-1, WS-1

Overboard Anything put over the side of a vessel, especially into the water. (X) Earlier, the term was in two words. WO-1

Overhang The ends of a craft that extend beyond her waterline. (e. XVIII p.e.) The origin appears to be early Dutch, *overhangen*, of the same meaning. WO-1

Overhatted Carrying too much sail, particularly pertaining to square-riggers. (XIX p.e.) Obviously a colloquialism, mostly British. K-2, DE-3

Overhaul (1) To slack or backhaul a line or tackle. (XVI) (2) To repair. (XVIII p.e.) (3) To overtake. (XVII p.e.) The origin in all these senses is vague at best. DE-3

Overhead The shipboard equivalent to the ceiling in a house ashore. (XIII) (See *Ceiling*) DE-3

Overwhelmed Overpowered. (XVI) Whelm, an early English word, comes from the Middle English *whelmen*, overturn. W-1, WO-1

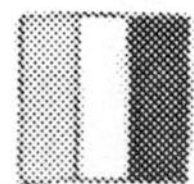

Oxter Plate (also *Oxter Plank*) The shellplate or planking that connects to the sternpost. (XIX p.e.) The origin of the term is debatable, but it appears to be an old one. It could be from Old English, *oxta*, armpit, or Old Norse, *ostr*, hollow of the neck — both implying the curves. P-1b, DE-5

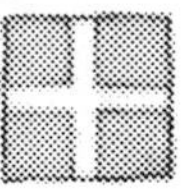

Packet A fast sailing vessel that had a regular, and sometimes scheduled run. (XVIII) The term is heard still, referring to the few remaining passenger ships on short routes in Northern European waters. The word goes back to Anglo-French, but probably is more directly derived from early French, *pacquet*, for any small, fast vessel. WO-1

Paddle A short oar-like device, used without a fulcrum such as an oarlock. (XII p.e.) The Middle English word was *padell.* S-2, DE-3

Painter A line in the bow of any small boat or ship's boat to secure or to tow it. (e. XVII p.e.) It came from *panter*, Old English for noose; thence from Old French, *pantierre*, snare; back to Greek, *pantheros*, catch; then to Sanskrit, *pankti*, a line. S-2, WS-1

Palm (1) The inner surface of the fluke of an anchor. (XVIII p.e.) (2) The face of an oar blade. (XVI) (3) A shaped leather strap for the hand, fitted with a wooden or metal disk, used to drive a needle when doing canvas and rope work. (XVIII p.e.) DE-3

Panama Chock A strong closed chock, or a chock that could be closed, usually on larger ships. (e. XX) It very probably got its name from its use, to keep a hawser or a towline in its chock with the changes of lead when a vessel is lowered in a lock, as in the Panama Canal. K-1

Parachute A type of "double-clewed" spinnaker used on racing sailboats. (XX) It obviously is named for its parachute-like shape when set and drawing. (See *Annie Oakley, Spinnaker*) R-2, WS-1

Parbuckle A type of hoisting purchase. (e. XVII p.e.) The origin is uncertain, but it is believed to have originated as a shipboard and shipyard term. An earlier spelling is parbunkel. S-2, WO-1

Parcel To cover or wrap a rope to protect from weather or from chafe. (e. XVII p.e.) The origin is probably Middle French, *parcager*, to wrap up. WO-1

Parrel (also *Parral*) (1) A sliding ring, usually with wooden beads, on the jaws of a gaff to allow it to move easily on its mast. (XVIII) (2) A ring to hold a square yard firmly to its mast. (XV p.e.) The term comes from Middle English, *pariel,* aphetic of appareel; the connection in these meanings is obscure. S-2, DE-3

Part As a verb, the mariner's word for break. (XIV) The word comes, via Middle and Old English, from the Old French, *partir*, one meaning of which was break. M-2, WO-1

Partners Reinforcing beams under the deck to lend strength and support where masts, bitts, capstans, other deck structures and deck openings are located. (XIII) The term earlier was *partenere*, and came from Old French, *panteiere*, support. S-1, WO-1

Pass (1) To throw or hand out a line. (XV) WO-1 (2) To run a line through a block or fairlead, or around a capstan, winch, or bitts. (XIII) DE-3 (3) To "pass the word" is said to have started its career on shipboard. (XV) DE-3 The word came, via Middle English, from Old French, *passer*, to pass.

Passaree (also *Passeree*) There are two definitions for this term, both applying to square-riggers: a studding sail clew outhaul, or the clew downhaul for a course. (XVII p.e.) The origin is French, *passaresse*, passer; it may have been the French name for certain running rigging. F-1, DE-3

Passenger was originally a sea term, referring only to those on ships. (XIV) The term came from Old French, *passager*, of this meaning, and it from Latin, *passare*, right of passage (aboard ship). WO-1

Paunch Mat A heavily reinforced mat of canvas to prevent chafe aloft and to patch hull damage. (e. XVII p.e.) It is derived from Old French, *pance*, chest armor. M-2, DE-5

Pavisade A canvas screen along a vessel's rail, a term now rarely seen. (XVI) Earlier it was an arrangement of shields along the sides, for protection from weather and weapons, also simply for stowage; this last use dated from Viking days. It came from Old French, the same word, and goes back to Latin, *pavensis*, shield. DE-3

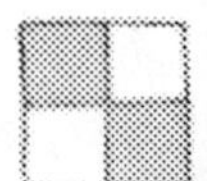

Pay (1) To let a line run out. (XV p.e.) This is from Old French, *payer*, of this meaning. WO-1 (2) To fill or patch a seam with pitch, as in caulking. (XVII) The term in this sense came also from Old French, *peier*, of the same meaning; it from Latin, *picare*, pitch. WS-1

Peajacket A short jacket of heavy wool worn for several centuries by sailors; in the services a short overcoat. There are two possibilities for this origin; one, from Britain, that they were made from "pilot cloth," a heavy water repellent wool, hence "P"; the other is the Dutch word *pij*, pronounced pea, a similar material used by Dutch mariners and shoresiders for many years. (p. XVI) (See *Reefer*) WO-1, WS-1

Peak (1) Of a fore-and-aft gaff sail, the outer end of the gaff and the upper and after corner of the sail. (XVII p.e.) (2) A compartment in either extreme end of a vessel, bow or stern. (XVIII p.e.) For the sail, the origin is French, *pic*, top or peak; for the spaces, the same word, but with the meaning of pointed, or thin. M-2, WO-1

Pelican Hook A type of slip hook. (XVIII p.e.) It got its name from the shape of the hinged bar that is part of the device—like a pelican's beak. DE-5, JR

Pelorus Also known as a dummy or dead compass, an instrument for taking bearings. (p.e. XIX) The derivation is uncertain, but a romantic supposition is that it was named to honor the pilot who got Hannibal around hazardous Cape Faro, Sicily, in 204 B.C. The cape was once known as Cape Pelorus. K-1, DE-4

Pendant (1) The old word, still sometimes heard, for a tapered flag or a long narrow one. (p. VIII) (2) Usually pronounced pennant, any of a variety of short lines with a block or a thimble spliced into one end. (XVII p.e.) The word came from Middle English and Middle French, the same word and probably the same meanings. M-2, WO-1

Penny The long-known designator for the sizes of nails. (p. XV) It referred to the price for one hundred nails, obviously relating to size. The term got its start in British shipyards and chandleries. S-1, JR

Periplus An old term for sailing directions, the first of which were written in Greece (ca. 350 B.C.) for the Mediterranean. (XVI) The word comes virtually intact from Greek, of the same meaning. S-1, DE-1

Petty Officer (1) Any of a variety of specially trained and rated enlisted men and women in the Navy and Coast Guard, as also in other navies. (p. XVII) (2) A senior unlicensed member of a merchant ship's crew. (e. XVI p.e.) The word comes from the French *petit*, in this sense secondary or subordinate. It is said that good petty officers are the backbone of a good ship. S-1, DE-3

Pier A structure extending into a harbor from the shore, alongside of which vessels can lie. (XIV) One scholar writes that the term implies greater length than wharf. The origin is Old English, *per*, coming through Middle English, *pere*, both of the same meaning. DE-3

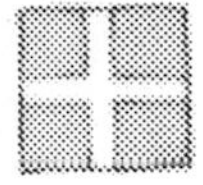

Pig Ballast for ships, in the form of cast metal, usually lead or iron blocks. Pigs were poured and cast in a form called a sow. (XVI) WW-1

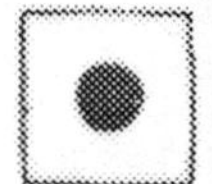

Piggin A small bucket-shaped hand bailer. (XVI) The origin of this term is uncertain; it appears to have come from Gaelic. DE-3

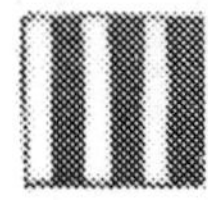

Pigsty Rail (also ***Pigsty Bulwark***) A high rail or bulwark with open planking, hence good drainage. (XVII) Still seen on many fishing vessels, the original purpose was as the name implies, to allow wave action to keep the decks well washed down where livestock was penned —either cargo or meat on the hoof. L-4

Pillow A part of the bracing structure at the inboard end of the bowsprit of a sailing vessel. (e. XVII p.e.) The derivation is late Old English, *pyle*, of this same meaning. S-2, DE-3

Pilot (1) Now generally a master mariner with special expertise who guides ships into, out of, and through bays, harbors, canals, and rivers. Formerly and rather vaguely, an officer who was in charge of a ship's maneuvers. (XV) (2) One name for a book of instruction and data for a specific area. (See ***Rutter***) The term came from Old French, *pedot*, thence via Latin, from the Greek *pedotes*, steersman. DE-3

Pinch To head a sailing craft too close to the wind, so that her sails are not fully effective. (XVIII p.e.) The word is probably a colloquialism. DE-4

Pink An old term for a craft that had much rake or that was "sharp-ended"; also of a British coastal vessel with these characteristics. (XV) (See ***Pinky***) DE-5

Pinky An old type of New England fishing schooner which had a sharp stern and narrow, long counter, and usually heavily raked masts. (XVII) The term may be from the Dutch *pinche*, meaning narrow. WO-1

Pinnace Earlier, a small ocean-going sailing vessel; later, any of a variety of ship's boats. (XVI p.e.) The derivation appears to be Old French, *espiance*, for small boat; it also could be early French, *pinasse*, something built of pine, ergo of light construction. It may also have come from early Italian, *pinacia*, a type of small boat. S-2, WO-1, WAB

Pintle The hinge pin on a rudder. (XV) The term came from Middle English, *pintel*, of the same meaning, and probably came into being shortly after the advent of stern rudders. One of the meanings of the word was pin. (See *Gudgeon*) S-2, WO-1

Pirate A sea-going renegade or robber. (XV) The word goes back, via French, to the Greek *peirates*, attack. WO-1

Pissdale (also *Pisdale*) A place on deck where sailors and officers "went"; a special scupper for the purpose located in the ship according to the rank of the user. (XIII) The key word was at one time not impolite to use; it came from Old France. Dale came from the Old Norse word *dael*, meaning among other things a hole or groove. P-2, DE-3

Pitch (1) The fore-and-aft motion of a vessel. (XV) The term in this sense is from Middle English, *pieche*, of the same meaning, and could go back to Old English. (See *Scend*) WO-1 (2) The pine tar used to caulk and otherwise preserve the wood and cordage of older wooden vessels. (VIII) This came from Old English, *pic*, and goes back to the Greek *pissa*, pine tar. WO-1 (3) A term to define the angle of a propeller blade to its axis. (XIX) The word itself probably came from the Middle English *picchen*, angle. DE-4, WO-1

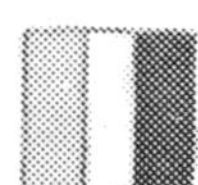

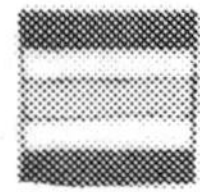

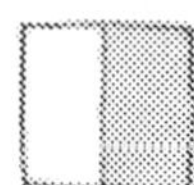

Pitometer (also called *Pitot Tube* and *Pit Log*) A device for indicating a vessel's speed through the water. (1. XIX) It was named for Henri Pitot, a French physicist who developed the principle for measuring water pressure by which it works. DE-4

Plait To braid small stuff into a mat or strop, for utilitarian and ornamental purposes. It is sometimes called *Plat* and often so pronounced. (XVIII p.e.) The word comes intact from Old French, and could go back to the Latin *plictum*, fold. L-4

Plane Sailing (also *Plain Sailing*) A method of plotting a course, referring principally to longitude coverage. (XVI) This was a technique believed to have been developed by Mercator. (See *Mercator*) K-1, DE-3

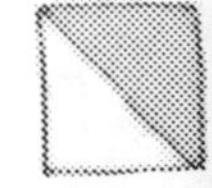

Plank A length of trimmed timber fastened to the frames to form the "skin" of the hull of a wooden vessel; also one fastened to the deck beams for the decks. (XIII) The word comes from the Middle English *planke*, of the same meaning, which is believed to have had principally a nautical connotation in that era. It goes back to Latin, *planka*, board. S-1, WS-1

Plate A section of sheet metal; a part of the skin, decks, or bulkheads of a steel or iron vessel. (XIV) Iron and steel ships did not appear until the XIX century of course, but metal was used much earlier for sheathing and other purposes. The derivation in the nautical sense is obscure. DE-4

Pledge (also *Pledget*) A thin roll of oakum used in caulking. (XVI) The term comes from late Latin, *plagella*, a plug for a wound. B-6, WO-1

Plimsoll Mark The marking on the side of any ocean-going vessel, indicating the depths or drafts to which she may be legally loaded under various conditions. (l. XIX) It was named after Samuel Plimsoll, a British "M.P.," who was very much involved with safety at sea and who was responsible for the regulation being enacted into law in 1876. It has long been international in scope. DE-1, WO-1

Plot (1) To lay out a vessel's course, her position or relevant data, or that of an objective or obstacle. (2) The result of plotting. (XVI) The term goes back through Middle English, to Old English, *platte*, of the same general meanings. WS-1, DE-3

Point (1) Nobody uses the points of a compass any more, but it used to be the only way. There are thirty-two, each of 11.25° of arc. (XVI) (See *Cardinal Points*) WO-1 (2) A sailing craft points well if she sails well when close to the wind. (XVIII p.e.) WO-1 (3) To point a line has two meanings: one is to taper the end (p. XVII), and the other is to have it ready, as a mooring line to pass ashore. (p. XIX) The word goes back to Latin, but probably not in a nautical sense. A-3, DE-3

Pontoon A static floating device. (XVII p.e.) This word goes back to Latin in much the same sense as one of its current uses, *ponto*, a bridge of boats. DE-3

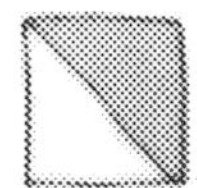

Poop (1) The high after-deck of yesteryear's ship, now much the same meaning for any raised deck in the stern section of a modern one. (XV) The origin, via Middle English, *poupe*, French and Italian, is the Latin *puppim*, the after section of a ship. This word, in turn, came from *puppis*, for doll or small image. It was a custom of the Romans and their predecessors to have a sacred image or idol mounted in the stern. (2) To be pooped, at sea, is to have a sea break over the stern, or over the poop. (p. XVII) S-1, WW-1

Poppets (1) The supports in a cradle or slipway for the ends of a vessel. (XVIII) DE-3 (2) The wood supports for oarlocks or thole pins on a pulling boat. (p. XVI) The term appears to come from the Middle English *popet*, one meaning of which is prop. DE-3

Port (1) A harbor city or town. (XIV) The origin is Latin, *portus*, port. The Old French, Old English and Middle English words were all *port.* S-1, WS-1 (2) The left side of any craft when facing forward. (XVII p.e.) Until the XIX century the usual term was larboard. Because of the obvious risk of confusion in orders from the similarity of sound of "starboard" and "larboard," the latter was legally and officially changed to "port" by the U.S. Navy in 1846, and a bit earlier (1844) by the British. The apparent reason for the choice of the word was the connotation of larboard—the loading, ergo the port, side. It may be interesting to note that in Captain John Smith's *Grammar*, the word port was used in this sense (1627). (See *Larboard*) DE-3, K-1, M-2, M-5 (3) An opening in the side, rail, or bulwark of a ship. (XIV) In this sense, the word came from Middle English and Old French, *porte*, and goes back to the Latin *porta*, a gate or an opening. S-2, WO-1

Porthole (also ***Portlight***) (XVII p.e.) (See *Port*) WO-1

Posh Swanky, luxurious. (XIX ?) The story goes that, in the days of the liners that ran to India and the Orient from England, the most desirable and more expensive staterooms were on the port side outbound and the starboard homebound, each being the cooler side of the ship in the usual hot conditions for a large part of the voyage; hence P.O.S.H.

Some say this is just a pretty story. One contention is that it was a corruption of P.O.S.N., the initials of the Pacific & Oriental Steam Navigation Co. The "P. & O." was a principal line on that route. Another explanation is that it simply was an English slang word for anything luxurious or fancy. V-1a, WM-3

Pram (1) In modern times a small yacht tender, with a squared bow. (XX) (2) A small workboat. (XVI) The origin is Middle Dutch, *praem*, workboat. WO-1

Pratique License or permission for a merchant ship to enter port and use its facilities. (XVII) Earlier the English spelling was prattick. The term comes from the French, the same word, of which an old meaning was interchange. WW-1

Prayerbook A small holystone, also sometimes called a Bible. It no doubt got its name from its relative size, also from the pious position required for its use. (p. XVIII) (See *Holystone*) JR, USN

Preventer A line, length of wire, or a tackle temporarily rigged to add strength, to relieve, or to prevent damage to running or standing rigging or other gear. (e. XVII, p. XV) The word came from Latin, *praeveire*, one meaning of which was to guard against. When it became a sea term is not known. DE-3, S-2

Pricker A small marlinespike or fid. (XVII p.e.) Earlier it was a gunner's tool as well as a boatswain's. DE-3

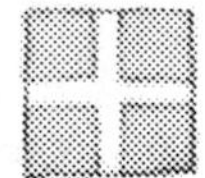

Proof Among other things, a standard of alcoholic content of liquor. It is mentioned here as it is believed in this meaning to have originated with the testing of cargoes of rum by customs and excise officers at dockside. A sample was taken, put in a dish and touched with a match. If "up to proof," about 50 percent by volume, it would ignite. The technique probably dates from the XV century, and was in use until the advent of the hydrometer in the late XVII. The word comes from Old French, *preuve*, prove, and goes back to Late Latin, *proba*, test. (*Proba*, is also a modern Russian word of this same meaning.) DE-3, JR

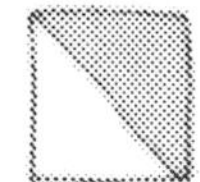

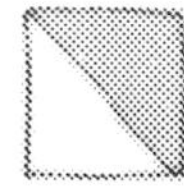

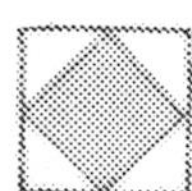

Propeller Also called a screw, it hardly needs definition. (XIX) The word is taken from Latin, *propellere*, to drive forward. WO-1

Prow An old and now poetic word for the bow structure of any craft. (XVI) The word comes from Old French, *proue*, and goes back to the Greek *proira*, bow of a ship. WO-1

Pudding Earlier called puddening, it is padding or protective netting to absorb shock and reduce chafe. (e. XVII p.e.) The origin is uncertain, but there are two possibilities, both of which could be right: Middle English, *poding*, sausage, and Old English, *puduc*, swelling. S-2, DE-4

Pulpit A railed structure at the bow or on the bowsprit, or simply a rail forward for safety. (XIX) Common to certain fishing craft, especially swordfishermen, earlier, the device began to appear on yachts in the 1940s, and is now almost universal equipment on these craft. The word comes, via Middle English, from Late Latin, *pulpitum*, a platform or stage. DE-4

Pungy A working and fishing boat common to the Chesapeake Bay. (XVIII) The word is probably a corruption of the Chippewa Indian word *tompung*, sledge. M-1, WAB

Punt A small, square-ended, flat-bottomed work boat of many uses. The word comes intact from Old English, also from Early Anglian, *pontebot*, a workboat. WO-1

Purchase (1) A tackle. (XVI) (2) Workable mechanical advantage. (XIII) The word comes from the Middle English *purchasen*, of this sense, and it from Old French, *porchacier*, one meaning of which was to gain. DE-3

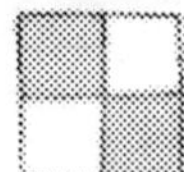

Purser A clerical officer in a merchant ship, who is in charge of her documents, accounts, and payroll; also a seagoing hotelman in a passenger ship. Earlier he was a low-ranking naval officer who was in charge of all stores. (XV) The term goes back, via French, to Latin, ***bursariar***, burser. WW-1

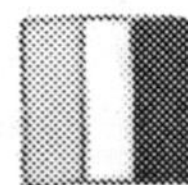

Puttocks An earlier name for *futtock shrouds.* (e. XVII p.e.) The origin is obscure; it may be a corruption of futtock. S-2, DE-3

Quadrant An old instrument for measuring the altitude angle of a celestial body. Its arc was not 90° but 45°, so it appears to be another name for an octant. (XVII) It could measure angles to 90°. (2) A curved yoke of 90° of arc that controls a rudder as a tiller. (m. XIX) The word is taken from Latin, *quadrans*, one quarter.

Quarantine Now the short routine delay of a merchant ship for entry into a port for acceptance of her documents, etc.; earlier the delays were longer, contingent sometimes on lengthy negotiations. (XVII) The term comes from Old French, and from the Latin *quadragesima*, The Forty Days. WS-1

Quarter A term for a bearing. ''On the quarter'' means 45° on either side from dead astern. (XVI) It apparently had reference to the quarterdeck. DE-3

Quarterdeck Now an area on a naval vessel reserved for ceremonies and honors, located on the ship wherever the comanding officer dictates; formerly it was a high partial deck aft, from which a ship was conned, and which sheltered the quarters of the afterguard and passengers. (p. XVI) K-1, WO-1

Quartermaster Now a rating in the sea services and to a lesser extent in merchant ships, for a petty officer who assists in the functions of the bridge, and earlier, of the quarterdeck. Formerly he was the man in charge of stores and other accessories below and on deck. (XVII p.e.) The origins seem apparent. WO-1

Quarters A general term for accommodations aboard ship. (XVI) It is uncertain whether this originally was a military or a maritime term. The origin in this broad meaning is not certain; it possibly had reference to a section of a community. DE-3

Quay A shoreside structure, usually of masonry, and parallel to the shoreline, serving as a berth or berths for craft of all sizes. (XIV) Common in European waters, it is pronounced like key, which becomes obvious when we find that the word came from the Middle English, *key*, of the same meaning, thence probably from the Breton word *kae*, an enclosure. WO-1

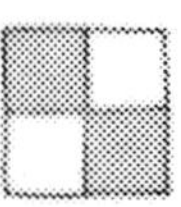

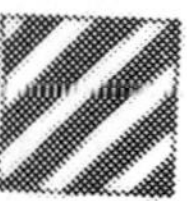

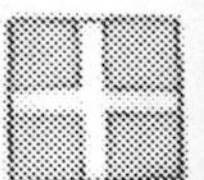

Rabbet A recess cut into a timber to accommodate another. (e. XVII, possibly XV) Common among shoreside carpenters today, it is believed to have been exclusively a shipbuilder's term. It appears to have come from the Old French *rabbat*, recess. M-2, WO-1

Rack (1) On earlier sailing ships, a framework at the bow, fitted with sheaves as fairleads for lines to the headsails. (XVIII p.e.) The word comes from Middle English. WS-1 (2) A nickname for a bunk on a naval vessel (which in some ships isn't much more than that). (XX) JR

Racking Fastening two opposing parts of a tackle together to keep it from moving. (XVII p.e.) The origin is obscure; it may be Old English or Middle Dutch. F-1, DE-3

Radar Electronic equipment for detecting range and bearings of objects and other ships. (m. XX) The term is an acronym for "RAdio Direction And Range." N-4

Raddle Small stuff or yarn woven or sewed into gaskets, gripes, or mats, either for added strength or as protection from chafe. (XVIII p.e.) Its origin is obscure, possibly Anglo-French. S-3, DE-5

Raffee (1) A sail set from the truck and the highest yard of a square-rig mast, usually triangular but sometimes four-cornered, and having its own jackyard. (XIX p.e.) (2) The name sometimes given to a vertically-divided fore-course set to a yard for running, on a schooner. The origin of this term is obscure, possibly Hindi. DE-3, JR, WWT

Raft Any of a variety of floating objects, formerly rigid but now often air-filled. (XV) The term comes from Middle English intact. It goes back to Old English *rapir*, and to Old Norse *raefer*, a supporting beam, rafts then being built of beams or logs. WO-1

Rail (1) The edge of a bulwark (XIII) (2) The upper and outer edge of the hull of a craft having no bulwarks. (XIX p.e.) (3) A system of pipe, wirerope, or rope, to keep people on board. (XIX) The term goes back to Old French, *reille*, via Middle English, *rail*. The French origin may not have been a nautical one. S-1, WS-1

Raise To come within visible distance of another vessel or an object, such as a buoy or a point ashore. (XVI p.e.) The word appears to have come from Middle English *reisen*, in turn from Old Norse, and meaning to come in sight of. M-1, DE-3

Rake (1) The earlier meaning referred to overhangs of a ship. (e. XVII p.e.) A more recent, and the current meaning is the degree of slope from the vertical for masts, funnels, and other tophamper of a ship. In the first sense the term probably came from Middle English, *ragen*, of that meaning; in the second, also probably Old English, *racian*, to take direction. S-2, DE-3

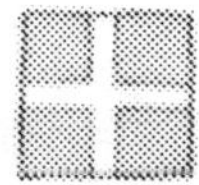

Ram An old term for the over-all length of a boat. (XVII p.e.) Its origin is obscure; it may be Old Norse. DE-3

Ramboline (See *Romboline*)

Range (1) The distance to another ship, a target, or a point ashore, etc. (XVI) (2) The range of a lighthouse, lightship, or a light buoy is the distance at which the light is visible. (XVII) (3) Two or more objects, such as beacons or lights, arranged in a line, called a range, by which to steer a safe course, as through a channel. (XVI) (4) A verb, to haul out a hawser or anchor cable for inspection or repair. The word in all these senses is believed to have come from the Old French, *reange*, range. WO-1

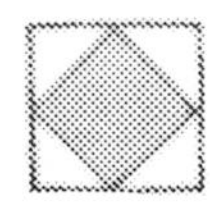

Rap Full Said of the sails when sailing close to but not hard on the wind, when they are well filled. (XIX p.e.) The derivation is uncertain, but it could be from Middle High German, *rap*, quick. S-3, DE-3

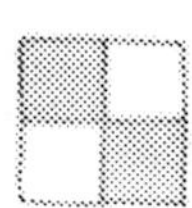

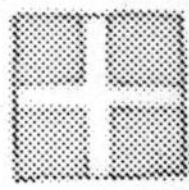

Ratlines (also ***Ratlins, Rattlings***) The rungs between the shrouds for going aloft, earlier of rope, now either rope or rods. (XV) Another and earlier spelling was raddlelines, and the Middle English source word was ***radelyne***, so there may be a connection with the word raddle. S-2, WO-1

Rattle (See ***Rattling Down***)

Rattling Down was the term for securing the ratlines to the shrouds. (XVII p.e.) The term appears to be a corruption of ratline. The process was done by starting at the upper deadeyes and working upward. S-2, WO-1, WAB

Rave Hook A tool for clearing (reaming out) oakum and pitch from seams. (XVI) The origin of the term is obscure; it possibly is Old Norse. P-1b, S-3, WAB

Raymond Hook A type of quick-release hook on a boat fall to free a boat quickly when waterborne. (l. XIX) It is named for its inventor, who, we are told, was a chief boatswain in the U.S. Navy. K-2

Razee A warship of the XVII or XVIII century which was reduced in size and weight by one deck. The assumption is that this was to increase speed. The origin of the term is French, ***vaisseau rasé***, loosely a cut-down ship. WW-1, DE-5

Reach (1) A point of sailing on which the sheets are eased, roughly with the wind abeam. (XVII) The term came from the Anglo-Saxon word ***raecen***, reach, but whether in this sense is uncertain. M-1, M-2, WO-1 (2) A fairly straight stretch of navigable water between bodies of land or between bends in a river or channel. (XVIII p.e.) In this sense the term appears to come from early Dutch. M-2, WO-1

Red Duster The "Red Ensign" of the British and some Commonwealth merchant services. Formerly one of three naval ensigns, it was designated for merchant vessel use in 1864. We do not know how this nickname came about, but it almost certainly was after the flag took on its new purpose. (l. XIX) K-1

Reef (1) A verb, to reduce the area of a sail exposed to the wind; the noun is the portion of the sail that can be folded out of use and the result of doing so. (XIV) The Middle English word was *riff*; the origin the early German *reff*, a strip of sail. (2) A shallow ridge of rock or coral. (XVI) The origin is Old Norse, *rif*, of this same meaning. S-1, WO-1

Reefer A short, heavy wool jacket worn by sailors for many years. (XIX p.e.) It apparently got its name because it is short and convenient to wear aloft. (See *Peajacket*) DE-3

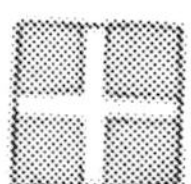

Reeming Iron A tool for cleaning out caulking in a seam. (p. XVI) It is a corruption of ream, and came from Middle English, *reme*, to open up. DE-3

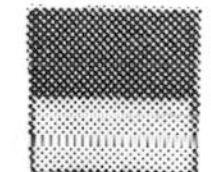

Reeve To pass a line through a block or fairlead. (XVI p.e.) An earlier spelling, reave, still is seen occasionally. Its origin is the Dutch *reven*, of the same meaning. S-2, WO-1

Regatta An occasion of boat racing. (XVIII p.e.) The word came from Italy, probably Venice. It is thought to be a corruption of the Italian word *rigattare*, to wrangle, and also from the Spanish *regatear*, hassle. No comment. WO-1

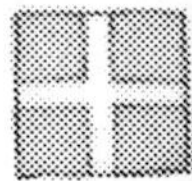

Register A general term, it is cited here as all vessels of most maritime nations are registered for legal and business purposes with various agencies, both government and civilian, the latter such as Lloyd's. (XVIII) The word comes directly from the Latin ***registrum***, record book. WS-1

Render To ease or free a line. (XVIII p.e.) The derivation is Old French, ***rendre***, to give back. S-3, DE-3

Rhumbline A course that crosses all meridians at the same angle. (XVII) A rhumb is a segment of arc, particularly on a compass, of 15°. The word appears to have come from the Middle French ***ryn***, a point of the compass. WO-1, WS-1

Rib Another word for frame, usually used in connection with small craft, earlier with larger ones too. (XIV) The origin is Old English, same word, same meaning. S-1, WO-1

Riband (also ***Ribband***) (1) A long longitudinal timber used in wooden boat and ship construction. (XVII p.e.) (2) Another name for water stripe. (l. XIX) The word comes from Old French, ***ruban***, ribbon. WO-1

Rig (1) The general term for the type of spar and sail arrangement of a boat or ship. (XV) (2) To equip a sailing vessel with sails, spars, and related gear. (XV) (3) To set any gear in readiness for a special purpose. (p. XV) The term comes from Old Norse ***rigge***, to arrange or prepare. M-2, WO-1

Right Sailing Running a course on one of the cardinal points of a compass, so as to alter only the latitude or the longitude. (XVIII) The word came from Anglo-Saxon; an early meaning, still inferred in mariners' language, is straight. K-1, M-1

Rigol The "eyebrow" over an air port. (XVI) The term is mostly British in use, and comes from French, *rigole*, a watercourse. (See *Eyebrow*) K-1, WO-1

Ringtail A trysail carried abaft or above the spanker on clippers and some later square-riggers. (XVIII) The origin of the term is not known; it may be that some of the early ones were made with an extra large clew cringle. DE-5, JR, KK

Rivet A bolt with the headless end hammered or pounded flat after insertion. (XIII) This was one technique for some of the fastening in Viking ships; however, the term came into English from the Old French *river*, to attach. WO-1, WS-1

Roach The curve on the after, or trailing, edge of a fore-and-aft sail or the foot of a square sail. (e. XVIII p.e.) The derivation is not known. F-1, DE-3

Roaring Forties Said of the band of latitude of 40° to 50° South, especially in the eastern hemisphere; also sometimes of the same north latitudes. (XVII) It is simply and appropriately named for lots of wind. K-1

Robands Pieces of line or yarn to secure square sails to their jackstays. (e. XVII p.e.) The term could be a corruption of rope band, or may have come from the Dutch *raband*, of that meaning—or both. (See *Jackstay*) M-2, WW-1

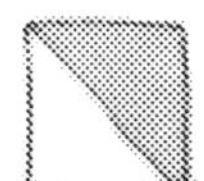

Rocker Bottom (also *Rocker Keel*) A craft's bottom or keel with a pronounced convex curve (XVIII p.e.) The word came from Old English, but probably not in this nautical sense. B-6, WAB

Rode The line to an anchor. (e. XVII p.e.) The term is believed to be a New England and Eastern Canadian colloquialism, possibly originating in Britain, a preterit of ride. M-2, DE-3

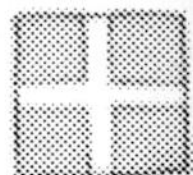

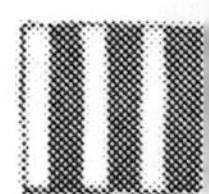

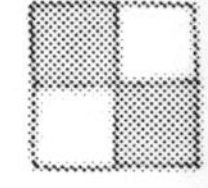

Rogue's Yarn Colored yarn passed around the contlines or woven into the strands of cordage. (XVIII p.e.) Utilized by the British and later the U.S. Navy, its original purpose was to discourage stealing. F-1, K-1

Rollock (also ***Rowlock, Rullock***) (See *Oarlock*).

Romboline (also ***Ramboline***) An old term for worn or condemned canvas and cordage, suitable only as chafing gear and for chinsing. (XIX p.e.) The term's origin is obscure, but it could be a corruption of rummage. DE-3

Rope One seagoing scholar writes, "That's the stuff lines is made from." Generally rope is all cordage over a certain size (in the Navy over one inch in circumference). (VIII) The word goes down the line —Middle English *roop*, Old English *rap*, Anglo-Saxon *rap*, and Old Norse *reip*, all meaning rope. Customarily only a few cordage items aboard ship are referred to as ropes; some of these are boltrope, bell rope, and manropes. (See the Appendix on ropes, also *Line*) M-2, DE-3

Rope Yarn Yarn made up of frayed rope fibers for a number of purposes, now largely obsolete. (e. XVII p.e.) S-2

Rope Yarn Sunday A half-holiday from regular work aboard ship, usually on Wednesdays—but never on Sunday—for the crew to work on their own gear and light odd jobs; an old naval tradition. (XIX) N-4

Roping Sewing a *boltrope* to a sail. (XVII p.e.) S-2

Rose Box The filter or strainer on the suction side of a bilge pump. (XIX p.e.) A good example of sailors' whimsy; you can imagine how roselike the scent and how petal-like the solid matter collected. (See *Strum Box*) M-1, N-4

Round (1) In shipbuilding, the shaping of the hull. (XVIII p.e.) (2) To turn a vessel into the wind or current, usually expressed to round up or to round to. (XVII p.e.) (3) To round down is an old term for seizing. (XVIII) S-2

Round House (1) The head for petty officers, on the beakhead. (XVI) B-4 (2) On later sailing ships, a compartment amidships for petty officers and apprentices. (XIX) K-1

Round Robin was first a seagoing and military expression. Robin was a corruption from the French word *ruban*, ribbon, a custom that travelled to England from France in the XVII century, when captains and other commanders had the right of inflicting severe punishment on the inciter of a grievance petition. Such petitions were signed by a number of officers or men, on a ribbon joined at its ends, so as to be endless and without a "first." Later the names of petitioners were in the form of a wheel. WM-3

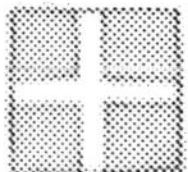

Rouse (1) To heave on a line. (XVIII p.e.) (2) To rouse the watch, or all hands, is to call them on deck, and to "bear a hand" is implied. (c. XVII p.e.) The term is probably a corruption of rise or arise. S-2, WS-1

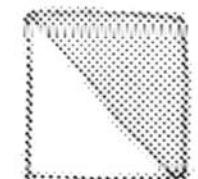

Row To propel a boat or ship by oars. (XIV) The word comes intact from Middle English, thence from Old Norse, *roa*, to row. WO-1

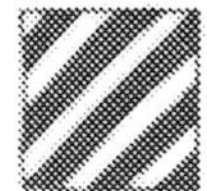

Rowlock (See *Oarlock*)

Royals The square-rigger's sails above the topgallants. Earlier they were the same. They got their current definition in the XVII century. The term may have come about from the concept that highest was best, hence regal or royal. S-1

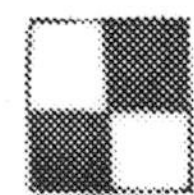

Rudder That all-important moveable fin aft by which any but the smallest craft is steered. (V) The earlier English term was *rother*, and applied to the steering oar. The first stern rudders were seen in the mid XII century. Probably the earliest English word was the Old English *roper*, from Old Norse, *roder*, a steering oar. WO-1, WS-2

Rummage An old term for the arrangement of casks in a vessel's hold, and later of any cargo. (XVI) The term is an aphetic of the Old French *arrumage*, arrangement, and has no reference to rum. The term rummage sale was originally for a dockside sale of unclaimed or unpaid-for cargo. DE-3, JR

Run (1) A point of sailing, that of being before the wind. (p. XIV) (2) The shape of the after end of the hull underwater. (e. XVII p.e.) (3) A passage of a vessel from one point to another or in a period of time. (XVII) The term in all senses appears to come from Old English, *rinnan* and from Old Fresian, *rinna*. S-2, DE-3

Runnel A wave trough caused by a tidal or other current close to shore. (XVI) The word comes from Old English, of the same meaning. WO-1

Runner (1) In sailing-ship days, and still alive, the term for a pendant with a tackle, for various purposes. (XVII p.e.) (2) The short name for running backstays on a fore-and-after. (XIX) DE-4

Running Rigging Applies to all the lines that can readily be moved, such as halyards, sheets, etc. (e. XVII p.e.) The term is still heard on cargo ships, as well as on sailing craft. M-2

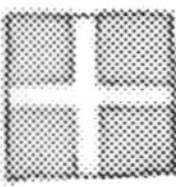

Rutter An early book of sailing instructions, mostly for coastal navigation. (l. XV) The first of these books were in French, compiled by a Pierre Garcie, and were entitled *Le Grand Routier*. The first English version appeared in the early XVI century. They were very thorough, and, we are told, very scholarly works. The term is an English corruption of *routier*, router, and obviously is taken from its predecessor. (See *Pilot*) K-1, DE-4

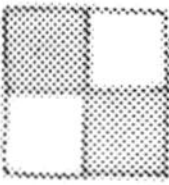

Sack Now commonly used ashore, this is a sailor's nickname for his bunk, and earlier for his hammock. (p.e. XIX) In the "old Navy" it had a very inelegant prefix. N-4, USN, JR

Saddle (1) a shaped bracket on a yard of a square-rigger to fit it to its mast. (2) Brackets on which studding sail yards rested, also on a square-rigger. (3) The seat of the jibboom on any sailing vessel. In all three definitions the term appears to occur in the XVII century; in the first possibly earlier. The word comes from Old English, *sadol*, saddle. S-2, DE-3

Sail hardly needs a definition either as a noun or a verb. (XI) It came in both forms from Anglo-Saxon, *segl*, of the same meanings, and appears in all modern Nordic languages in some recognizable form. The Modern German is the same as the Anglo-Saxon. M-2, WO-1

Sailor As for sail, little comment is needed, except that for some it applies to anyone who spends or has spent some time on the water. (XVI p.e.) an earlier spelling was *sayler*. The origin is the same as for sail. WO-1

Saint Elmo's Fire Light sometimes seen in the rigging at sea, caused by a static electricity discharge. (XV) St. Elmo is probably a corruption of St. Erasmus (ca. 300 A.D.), a patron saint of Mediterranean sailors. (See *Corposant*) B-1, K-1

Sally (1) To venture forth, as to sea. (XVI) The origin is the Old French *saillie*, sortie. (2) To cause a vessel to roll or rock, to work her loose if aground. (XVI) The derivation in this sense is probably Middle and Old French, *salire*, jump. DE-3

Saloon Generally the main cabin, or in passenger ships the dining room. (XVIII) It comes from the French, *salon*; and can be traced to Anglo-Saxon *sael*, hall; and to Gothic *salyan*. A modern corruption of the term is salon, a word which should be allowed to stay ashore. WO-1

Salvage Payment made for saving or assisting a vessel in trouble, or saving her cargo. (XVII) The name came direct from Old French, thence from the Latin *salvare*, to save. DE-3

Sampan A sturdy and simply constructed coastal, harbor, and river craft prevalent in the Orient. (XVII) The name is believed to have come from Cantonese, *san*, three, and *pan*, board, its earlier conventional planking. WS-1, DE-3

Samson Post (1) A single heavy bitt. (XVIII) (2) A mast to support cargo or boat cranes. (XIX) The origin of the term is uncertain; it could be a nickname after the strongman of biblical fame. DE-3

Saxboard An uppermost plank of an open boat—the gunwale strake. (XVII p.e.) The term appears to come from *sax*, an Old English and later a Middle English word for a type of woodworking tool. DE-3

Scandalize A term for shortening sail quickly. In a gaff-rigged vessel one good way is to lower the peak of a sail. (XVIII) Earlier terms were to scantle or to scantalize. the origin of the term is uncertain. It probably is a corruption of scant, in the sense of making smaller; or it may relate to *Scant*. The former seems more likely. WO-1

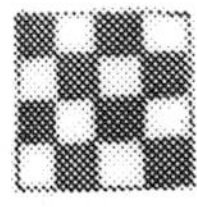

Scant An old term, said of the wind when a sailing vessel could just make her course good when close hauled. (XVI) The word came, via Middle English, from Icelandic, *scampt*, of the same broad meaning. WW-1

Scantlings (1) The dimensions of a vessel's structural members. (XVI) (2) A broad term for specifications to which a ship is built. (XVI) The term is from Old French, *escantillon*, a carpenter's and mason's—and possibly a shipbulder's—tool. WO-1

Scarf (also *Scarph*) The fitting of two timbers together by a bevelled joint. (XIV) The term goes straight back to Anglo-Saxon, *sceorfen*, of this meaning. It is an old technique, probably originating in boat and shipbuilding. S-1, WS-1

Scend (also *Send*) To pitch heavily. (e. XVII p.e.) The term appears to be an aphetic of one or two words, ascend or descend, depending on what a vessel's bow is doing at the time. The origins, via French, are Latin *ascendere* and *desendere*, rise and fall. (See *Pitch*) M-2, WO-1

Schooner A sailing vessel of two or more masts, the prevailing rig of which is fore-and-aft. (e. XVIII) An earlier spelling was scooner. The origin is not certain, but one story prevails: (ca. 1713) an observer of an early vessel so rigged commented, "See how she scoons!" *Scoon* is believed to be an early English and New England word for scud, which see.

One authority refutes this story, pointing out that a Dutch map of the New England coast dated 1657 showed a body of water called Schoone Havn, possibly now Plum Island Sound, near Newburyport, Mass., the connection of the terms being obvious; furthermore that the rig evolved prior to 1713. Some researchers claim the origin of the rig was British (ca. 1670), however that was apparently different from the American, having no headsails. The evidence is that the rig with which we are familiar is an American refinement. A-3, H-1, L-1, WAB

Sciatic Stay (See *Triatic Stay*)

Scope refers to the ratio of anchor chain or line let out to the depth of the water where anchored. (e. XVII p.e.) The derivation is not clear in this sense; it could be from early Italian. WO-1

Scotchman Chafing gear of leather or wood, in the standing rigging of a sailing ship. (p. XVIII) Also still used for certain chafing gear; it probably was a forecastle nickname, as a gear saver. P-1, DE-3

Scow (1) A square-ended, flat-bottomed craft. (XVIII) Smaller scows are used for workboats, the larger to transport goods. (See *Barge*) (2) A type of fast racing sailboat with blunted long ends, popular on our midwestern lakes. (l. XIX) The origin of the term in both senses is probably Dutch, *schouw*, a ferryboat, usually blunt-ended. WO-1

Scowing An anchoring technique by which a line is made fast to the anchor crown to facilitate breaking it out. (XVIII) The origin is obscure in this sense. H-2, WO-1

Scrimshander One who does scrimshaw work. A possibility for the origin of this word, and for that of scrimshaw, is the word *scrimshanker*, an old man-o'warsman's nickname for a shirker. This work was done, at least theoretically, on a man's leisure time. The concept may be a weak one, as most scrimshaw was done on whaling ships, where the crew had the raw materials. DE-3

Scrimshaw Etched drawing and carving of scenes and designs done on sperm whale teeth, whalebone, ivory, etc. (XIX p.e.) (See *Scrimshander*) DE-3

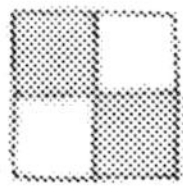

Scud (1) To run before the wind at good speed, some say with reduced sail. It came from Old English, *skyndan*, of that meaning. (2) Driving mist or low clouds in stormy weather. It is an old Scottish word, and may have come from Swedish, *skyde*, of the latter meaning. WO-1

Scull (1) To propel a boat with a single oar at the stern. (XVI) (2) A small very light and narrow racing rowing boat for one or two oarsmen. (XIX) (3) A light oar, now usually spoon bladed. (XIV) (4) Earlier, a small light rowing boat. (XVI) The origin appears to be the Middle English *sculle*, for the older senses and adopted for the newer. DE-3

Scuppers Drains for the weather decks. (XV) Earlier sometimes spelled skupper; the term came via Middle English from Old French, *escopier*, to bail or empty. S-2, WO-1

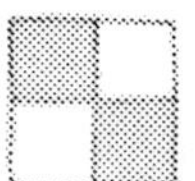

Scuttle (1) A small hatch or opening on deck. (XV) (2) The opening on the head of a cask, as for drinking water. (XV) The term in these meanings comes from Old French, *escoutille*, hatchway. (3) To sink a vessel by opening her seacocks or by cutting through the bottom. (XV) The origin in this sense may be the same as for the foregoing. S-1, WO-1

Scuttlebutt Shipboard rumors or gossip. (XIX p.e.) The scuttlebutt was a cask with scuttle, for drinking water and other potables, around which the men could be expected to gather and chat. The term is still used in the U.S. Navy for a drinking fountain. (See *Shaft Alley,* also *Butt*) WM-3, USN

Sea A definition seems unnecessary. The word came into Modern English via Middle English *see*, from Old English, *sae*, Old Norse, *saer*, and Anglo-Saxon, *sae.* It is recognizable in all the modern Teutonic tongues. WO-1

Seacock A through-hull valve below the waterline. (p. XVI) Cock is an old word for several types of valves, and comes from Middle English. DE-3

Seam The line or groove formed by abutting or overlapping edges of planks or plates. (X) It comes, through Middle English, *seme*, from Old English and Old Norse, *seam*, seam. A related word is Old English, *siwan*, meaning to sew. Seams of early vessels in Britain, and earlier yet in Scandinavia, were fastened with thongs: in effect, sewn. S-1, DE-5

Seaman goes back to Old English, *seamann*. (XII p.e.) As you might expect, the word is recognizable in the modern Nordic languages. WO-1

Sea Room The necessary space on the water for a vessel to maneuver safely. (XVI) W-2

Secure More generally used on shipboard than ashore, to make fast, to fasten securely, to cease. (e. XVII p.e.) The origin of the word is Latin, *securare*. DE-3

Seine A fishing net suspended in the water by floats on the surface, and weighted below, in use by 500 B.C. The word came, via Middle and Old English and Latin, from the Greek *sagene*, fishing net. DE-4

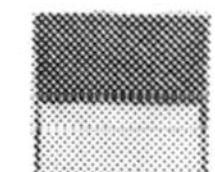

Seize To wrap with small stuff or with wire, as one line to another, a line to a spar, etc. (e. XVII p.e.) Its origin is early Modern or late Middle English, *seise*, which spelling is still seen in Britain. M-2, DE-5

Selvagee Small stuff or yarn, served or marled to make a strop. (XVIII p.e.) The term came via Middle English, from Middle Dutch, *selfegge*, self-edged. WO-1

Semaphore A system of visual signalling by daylight, believed to have been developed relating to marine traffic. (XVII) The word is adapted from the Greek *sema*, sign, and *phoros*, bearing. DE-5

Send To pitch. (See *Scend*)

Sennit (also *Sennet*) Braided small stuff of many varieties and uses. (e. XVII p.e.) One earlier purpose was to protect gear from chafe, hence the likelihood of the origin being the French *ecoussinet*, pad or mat. S-2, WW-1

Sentinel A weight suspended on an anchor cable to reduce shock whan a vessel is anchored in rough or turbulent water. (XVI) The origin in this sense is not known; the word comes from Latin, via early French. (See *Killick*) D-3, DE-3, JR

Serve (1) To wrap a line or wire to protect it from chafe or weather. (p. XVI) The derivation is probably Old French, *servir*, one meaning of which was to protect, and which came from Latin, *servare*, to preserve or protect. (2) To be a member of a ship's company, especially in the services. (XVI) The origin in this sense is Latin, *servire*, to serve in the sense of duty; and came to us via Old French and Middle English. S-2, DE-3

Set The direction in which a current or tidal flow, moves a vessel. (XVI p.e.) The word in this sense comes from Old French, *sette*, influence. B-6, DE-3

Sew (also *Sue*) (1) To ground a vessel at low tide. (2) The amount of tidal change needed to float a grounded vessel. (Both e. XVII p.e.) The word, now rarely heard, comes from the Middle French *essewer*, out of water. M-2, DE-4

Sextant A navigation instrument for measuring the angle of altitude of a celestial body. (XVII) The term comes from Latin, *sex*, six or sixth, and *ans*, part of. WO-1

Shack Earlier a colloquialism for any small deckhouse, it has come to mean a special compartment, such as the radio shack. (XIX p.e.) The term appears to have originated among mariners in the Caribbean and the Gulf of Mexico. Its origin is the Aztec word *xacalti*, meaning hut. WO-1

Shackle Any of a variety of connecting devices, most often roughly U-shaped, with a pin across the opening. (XV) The term comes from Old English, *scaacul*, link. WO-1

Shaft Alley (1) The tunnel for the propeller shaft, between the engine room and the stern. (2) Rumor or gossip in a merchant ship—it is a quiet area for the purpose. (XIX) (See *Scuttlebutt*) JR

Shanghai Enforced "volunteering" to raise a crew. The story is too long for this book, but the term originated on San Francisco's notorious Barbary Coast, where men were so recruited to man ships usually sailing in the China trade. (m. XIX) DE-3

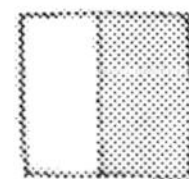

Shank The shaft of an anchor, between the ring or stock and the crown. (XVI) The word comes from Old English, *sceanca*, shaft. WO-1

Shanty (See *Chantey*)

Shape To lay out a course or a navigation plan. (XVI) The term probably comes from Middle English, *shapen*, thence from Old English, *skeppan*, to form. DE-3

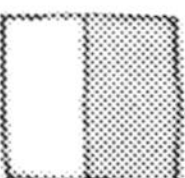

She Much has been said and written about why ships and boats are referred to in the feminine, and it all appears to be happy guesswork. Here are a few of the guesses: (1) A ship upon which one's life could depend was as near and dear as one's wife or mother. (2) A ship is as capricious, demanding, and absorbing as a woman. (3) The Greek goddess of navigation was Minerva, and in her honor all Greek ships were considered as feminine.

It may be interesting to note that another ship being watched from the bridge or cockpit is often spoken of as "he." This refers to the other skipper or watch officer rather than to the vessel, sometimes in wonderment as to what "he" is going to do next. WS-2, JR

Shears Long spars lashed together at the top, used to step or lift masts and to handle heavy gear and cargo on a sailing ship at dockside. (XVII) The term comes from Middle English, ***shere***, of the same meaning. DE-3

Sheathing Covering of the underwater part of the hull with extra material as protection from damage and fouling from various forms of marine life. (XVII p.e.) Ships were sheathed in the XII century and possibly before, earlier with special woods, then sheet lead, and later sheet copper. The word comes from Old English, ***sceath***, meaning sheath. M-2,WP-1c

Sheave The roller in a block. (XIV) Earlier spelled shiver, the Middle English word was ***sheeve***. The origin could have been early Dutch, ***schiff***, or Old English, ***skive***, or both, each meaning pulley. The reason the term is pronounced "shiv" probably relates to ***shiver***. S-2, WO-1

Sheer (1) The curve of the profile decklines of any craft. (XVII p.e.) (2) A sudden sharp change of course. (XVI) (3) The angle a craft takes to her anchor and its cable. (e. XVII p.e.) (See *Grow*) The term is believed to come from Old English, but the derivation is obscure. WO-1

Sheerpole A wooden and later metal bar across the feet of the shrouds, serving as a spreader and as the lowest step aloft. (XVIII p.e.) The origin in this sense is obscure. B-6, L-1, S-3

Sheet A controlling line to a sail. (XIII) The term comes from the Old English word *skeatline*, of this same meaning, and could go back to Old Norse, *skaut*. S-1, WO-1

Sheet Anchor The heaviest anchor on board older ships, for use in heavy weather. (XV) The books say the derivation is *sheten*, Middle English for shoot, intimating handling quickly. This hardly makes sense, it being the heaviest and largest. The term more likely came from the Old English *skeat*, a platform, as this anchor was usually stowed abaft the forecastle deck, and often secured to it. WO-1, JR

Sheets (See *Stern Sheets*)

Shell (1) The outer plating of the hull of a steel or iron ship. (XIX) (2) The sides of a block. (XVII) Also called the cheeks. The word in these senses probably comes from Old English, *skill*, shell-shaped or shell. DE-5, WS-1 (3) a very narrow racing boat for four to eight oarsmen. (XIX) In this sense the term probably refers to its very thin shell-like planking.

Shellback (1) An old experienced sailor, a nickname of uncertain origin, which could refer to the lack of fancy bathing facilities in the forecastle. (2) Any mariner who has crossed the equator, and who has been inducted into the "Ancient and Honorable Order." The custom of celebrating "crossing the line" is said to have originated with the Vikings, who did so on crossing various parallels on their voyages. L-8

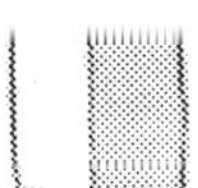

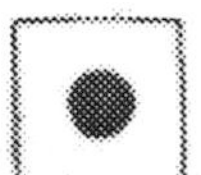

Ship A broad term describing any large ocean-going vessel (VIII) In sailing-ship days it defined a specific rig, of three or more masts, all square rigged. (e. XVIII p.e.) The origin of the word is obscure, as the original root is not known. It was seen in various similar forms in all the old Nordic languages, and is recognizable in all the modern ones. (See *Boat*) WO-1

Shipping Articles (See *Articles*)

Shipshape Said of any craft that is orderly, neat, well maintained, and properly fitted out. (p. XVI) (See *Bristol Fashion*) DE-3

Shole A flat timber or piece of metal placed under the keel or shores when a vessel is drydocked or hauled out; also a shoeplate to protect the rudder. (e. XVIII p.e.) Also seen as sole, it appears to have the same origin. S-3, JR

Shores (1) Braces to hold a vessel upright when in drydock. (XIV) S-1 (2) Supports for damaged parts of a ship's hull. (XV) S-2 (3) Braces to prevent cargo or stores from moving or shifting. (XVI p.e.) The derivation is Middle Dutch, *schore*, support. WO-1

Short Stay Said when the anchor chain or cable is "up-and-down" but the anchor is still on the bottom, in the process of hoisting. (e. XVII p.e.) The origin of the term is probably the same as that for long stay, which see. D-3

Shot A length of anchor cable, later of chain.(XIV) The derivation is obscure. It may be from Dutch, *schoot*, rope, or from French, *escoute*, a kind of cable; also shoot is an old English word for splice. DE-3 (2) The act of getting a sextant angle (and the time) of the sun or a star. (XIX p.e.) WO-1

Shove Off To push away, hence colloquially to leave. (XII) The derivation is probably *scufan*, Old English for push. WW-1

Shrouds The major side stays of a mast. (XVI) The term as used ashore came from the shipboard sense; the shrouds were heavily wrapped for their protection from the elements. The derivation of the word is somewhat uncertain, but is probably Old Norse, *scruth*, for wrapping. S-1, WS-2

Sister (also *Sistering*) Added timbers, as fastened to a ship's frames or floors for extra strength. (XVII) The origin in the nautical sense is obscure; the word in the sense of support came from Old Anglian (XIII). B-6, DE-3,WO-1

Skeet A long-handled dipper of various uses. (XVII p.e.) The origin of the term is obscure; it was seen in the XV, but possibly not for shipboard gear. S-1, WO-1

Skeg Any of a variety of structures on a hull's bottom at or near the stern. (XIII) Earlier *skegg*, the word appears to come intact from Old Norse. S-1, DE-3

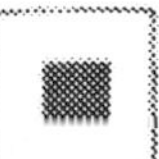

Skiff A small boat, now flat-bottomed. (XVI) Earlier, skiffs were more probably round-bottomed. They were the smallest of three boats normally carried by a ship. The origin is Old High German, *skif*, of the same meaning. S-1, WO-1, WAB

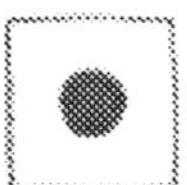

Skin The outer sides and bottom of any craft. There well may be a direct connection between the term and the fact that early craft in many parts of the world were built of animal skins over a wooden framework. N-5

Skipper A nickname for the captain; also, on smaller craft, especially yachts, the person in command. (XIV) The word comes from Middle Dutch, *schipper*, the captain of a small vessel. WO-1

Skylark Now hardly a sea term, it once was. It meant to romp in the rigging of a sailing ship, such as sliding down the crossjack stay. (XVIII p.e.) Lark in this sense comes from the Anglo-Saxon word *lac*, to play. L-4, N-5

Slablines (also *Slaplines*) Lines to trice up the foot of a course sail on a square-rigger, for better visibility ahead from the poop or quarterdeck. (XVIII p.e.) The word comes from the Dutch *slapjin*, of this meaning. F-1, DE-5

Slack Loose, relaxed, or free. (XVI) This term comes via Middle English from Anglo-Saxon and Old English, *slack* and *sleak* respectively, both meaning loose. W-2, WS-1

Slant (1) Also spelled slent, an old word for a light breeze. (XV) (2) The angle of a sailing craft's course relative to the direction of the wind. (XVII p.e.) Earlier it was sometimes seen as slaunt. The origin in both senses is Old Norse, *slent*, breeze. DE-3

Slewline A line for clearing an anchor cable that is fouled with another. (XVIII p.e.) It is sometimes called a clear-hawse, particularly in the Navy. Slew appears to be a corruption of slue, to turn. DE-3

Sliding Gunter (See *Gunter Rig*)

Slip A berth for any craft, between piers or floats. (XVI) The origin is early German, *slippe*, a cut. WO-1

Slip, To Give the To get away from something or someone. Originally this was a mariner's expression for an anchored ship hurriedly getting out of trouble by slipping her cable. (e. XVII p.e.) L-4

Slipping the Cable (1) To let out or cut, and buoy the anchor cable to get under way in a hurry. Yesteryear, hoisting the anchor was a long and slow process. (XVII p.e.) (See *Cut and Run*) S-1, DE-3 (2) A slang term for a sailor's dying. B-1

Slipway Tracks or a platform, inclined toward the water, for the keel blocks on which a ship is built and from which she is launched. (XVIII p.e.) F-1b, DE-3

Sloop (1) Now a one-masted fore-and-aft rigged sailboat. (2) Earlier (c. XVI) any of a variety of small sailing vessels of different rigs; for example, a sloop of war was usually ship-rigged. The derivation is not clear; it could be from the Dutch *sloep*, a vessel that sails well. WO-1

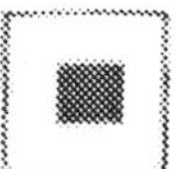

Slop Chest (1) Earlier, the source of supply aboard ship for clothing for the crew, especially for foul weather. (l. XVII p.e.) (2) Now a ship's canteen for personal necessities and comforts for a merchant ship's crew. Slop was, among other meanings, an early word for personal gear. It came from the Middle English word *sloppe*, of this meaning, and probably from Old English, *oferslop*, outer garment. DE-3

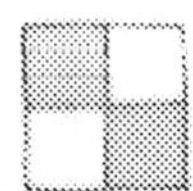

Slue (also *Slew*) To turn, or to slide, sharply and involuntarily. (XVII p.e.) The origin of the term is not known, but it did originate as a nautical term. WO-1

Slumgullion A stew for the crew's mess. (e. XIX p.e.) The derivation is not too appetizing; slum is an old word for slime, and gullion, English slang for stomach-ache. DE-3

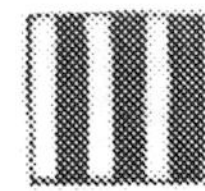

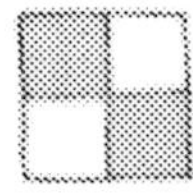

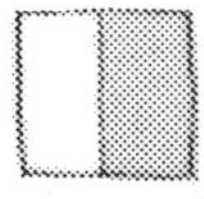

Slush (1) Grease rubbed on the masts, also on running-rigging wire and various equipment, as a heavy lubricant and preservative. (XVIII) (2) Grease and fats from the galley. (XVIII) The word is apparently a corruption of sludge. D-3

A slush fund—another expression that got its beginning at sea—was money raised by the sale of galley fats, the proceeds being used for "luxuries" for the crew. D-3

Smack A small coastal fishing vessel. This is not often heard in American waters. It came from Middle Dutch, *smake*, a type of boat, and may go back to Anglo-Saxon. WS-1

Small Stuff Any small cordage, such as marline, codline, spun yarn, etc. (XV) Stuff comes from Old French, *estoffe*, a word for material; it may go back to Late Latin. WO-1

Smelling A vessel's "feeling the bottom," to loose speed and good steering because of shallow water. (XIV) The word in this sense comes from early Middle English, *smellen*, to sense or feel. WO-1

Smiting Line A line to break out a sail that has been sent up in stops. (XVII p.e.) The word comes from Middle Dutch, *smiete*, a line attached to a sail. M-2, DE-3

Smoking Lamp Now mostly a naval term; when "lighted" the crew is permitted to smoke, and when "out" no one is permitted to do so. (XVIII p.e.) Earlier lamps were kept in various quarters on board, from which the men could light their pipes when a lamp was burning. L-4, N-4

Snake (See *Worming*)

Snake Line A line rove through grommets on the topmast shrouds of a square-rigger, for the same purpose as catharpins. (XIX) It was seen mostly on the later tea clippers. (See *Catharpins*) KK

Snatch Block A block with an opening on its side, to receive a line along its length. (e. XVII p.e.) The origin of snatch in this sense is uncertain; it may have been Middle Dutch, *snacken*, or Middle English, *snacchen*, to seize quickly. M-2, DE-3

Snorkel A device for a swimmer to breathe while under water. (m. XX) It got its name from modern German, *schnorkel*, the air intake on a WWII U-Boat, which permitted her to use diesel power while running at periscope depth, to save her batteries. N-4, JR

Snotter (1) A line and fairlead used to keep braces and sheets clear when yards were sent up or down on a square-rigger. (XVIII) (2) The becket at the heel of a sprit on a sprit-sail rigged boat. (XVII) (also *Snorter*) the derivation is obscure in both senses, but it is from a North Britain dialect. DE-4

Snow A two-masted square rigger like a brig, except carrying a jackmast close to and parallel to the mainmast, on which the spanker was rigged. (l. XVII) The word comes from the Dutch *snaauw*, their name for this rig. (See *Brig*) WO-1

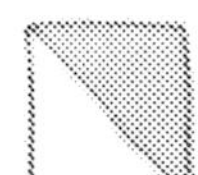

Snug Now a word in general use, this is another sailor's word that came ashore. It meant neat, trim, or compact, also tight. (XVII p.e.) It appears to come from early Danish, *snyg*, of the same general meaning. WW-1

Sole The decking of the cabin(s) of a smaller vessel, also called the cabin sole. (XIX p.e.) S-3, N-1, K-1

Sonar The acronym for underwater echo-ranging equipment, originally for detecting submarines by small warships. (SOund NAvigation Ranging). (m. XX) The British earlier called it ASDIC. N-4

Son of a Gun Originally a sea term. In sailing-ship days as late as the XVIII century, women were allowed aboard some warships, even at times at sea, the result of which was inevitable, ergo the early definition was obvious. One saying was "begat in the galley and born under a gun." K-1, JR

Soojee The act of washing down decks and topsides, and the tool by which it is done. (l. XIX p.e.) The word may have come from the Japanese *suji*, to clean. a longer word is soojie moogie. One scholar wrote that he found twenty different renderings of this term. (See *Squeejee*) DE-5

S.O.S. The old radio distress signal. (e. XX) Some say it meant "save our ship," but it is more probable that the letters were chosen because of the simplicity of the code—three dots, three dashes, and three dots. JR

Sound (1) To measure the depth of the water under a vessel. (2) To measure the contents in a ship's tanks and bilges. (Both XV) The origin is uncertain. It could be the French *sonder*, or Old English and Anglo-Saxon *sund*, both of which mean sound, perhaps in this sense. WO-1

Spanker A fore-and-aft sail usually carried aft on sailing craft, in various locations depending on the rig. (XVII) The origin is uncertain, but it could well have been Old English, *spank*, to move quickly. WO-1

Spar A pole in the rigging of any craft, such as a mast, boom, or yard. (XIV) The word comes from Old Norse, *sperra*, Anglo-Saxon *sparrian*, and Old French *esparre*, all of this meaning. WO-1

Spar Deck (1) Earlier, a partial deck in the waist of a sailing ship, and still earlier, of a galley. (XVI) (2) The upper deck, full or partial, of certain types of modern freighters. It got its name from its being where spare spars were stowed. L-4

Speak To hail or converse with another ship at sea. (e. XVII p.e.) One speaks a vessel, not to her. S-2

Spell To act for or to relieve a fellow seaman, as to spell the helmsman. (XVI) The origin of this term is the Anglo-Saxon *spelian*, to act for. S-2, WW-1

Spider An iron outrigger, to keep a line clear of other gear. (e. XIX) It may have got its name from its spindly appearance. WP-1c, DE-5

Spider Band A heavy iron ferrule around a mast, fitted with belaying pins. (l. XVIII) As with spider, it probably was named for its resemblance to the arachnid. (See *Fiferail*) DE-5, JR

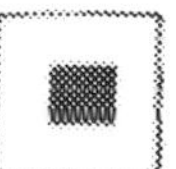

Spindrift Spray off the tops of waves, created by a strong wind. (XVI) It is a variation of the Scottish word *spendrift*, of the same meaning, and could go back to the Latin *spuma*, foam. DE-4

Spinnaker A large racing sail for modern yachts, for running and reaching. (l. XIX) The word is very probably a corruption of *Sphinx*, the name of a mid XIX century British schooner yacht that carried such a sail. Earlier names were Sphinxer and Sphinx's acre. L-4, WW-1, WAB

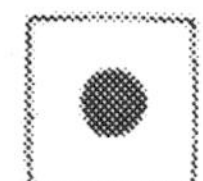

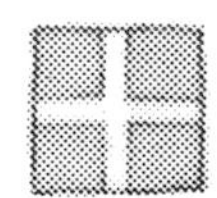

Spirketting Various strengthening timbers of old wooden ships, on the bows, under the decks, and between the floors. (XVII p.e.) The term may have come from the Old English, *spirce*, scatter, implying perhaps to spread the strain or stress. M-2, DE-4

Spitfire A small jib, also a storm jib. (XVIII) The origin is obscure, but implies defiance to high winds and heavy seas. S-3

Splice Joining together of two ropes or parts of one, by interweaving the strands. It was known to have been a skill of the Vikings in the VIII century. (XVI p.e.) The term probably came from early Dutch, *splissen*, of this same meaning. B-8,WO-1

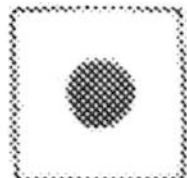

Splice the Main Brace Until recently the British Navy's custom of issuing grog to all hands, to celebrate an important event or accomplishment. (l. XVIII) The origin of the phrase is not known, and many guesses have been made. One I like is that when H.M.S. *Victory* was in dock and teaming with shoreside workers, some officers decided to go to the wardroom for a drink and chose to disguise their intent. Ergo the term was their code. N-4, JR

Sponson (1) Structural projections on the sides of various craft, also of flying boats, for extra buoyancy or stability. (2) Another name for a paddle box of a sidewheel steamer. (Both XIX) The term is probably a corruption of the word expansion. (See *Bustle*) WO-1

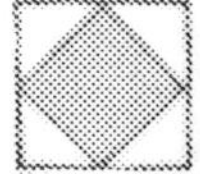

Spreaders This is an older term than is generally known. They are short horizontal spars to hold various stays in a desirable position or angle. (l. XVIII) On square-riggers they were usually diagonal to the centerline and abaft the crosstrees. On modern sailboats they usually are about athwartships. WS-1

Spring Line Now a mooring line at an acute angle to a vessel, as from the bow aft, earlier it also was a line from the anchor or its cable led well aft to enable a vessel to control her heading or sheer. (XVIII p.e.) F-1b, DE-3

Spring Stay A line or tackle to assist a regularly-rigged stay; a preventer. (XVIII) Also, another name for the *Triatic Stay*, which see. B-6, JR

Spring Tide A phase of the tidal cycle of maximum rise and fall. (XVI) The origin may be the Anglo-Saxon *springer*, bulge. DE-3

Sprit Any of several small spars used to spread certain sails, but usually a long spar set diagonally across a fore-and-aft sail to support its peak. (XIV) The derivation is both Anglo-Saxon and Old English, *spreot*, of broadly the same meaning. S-1, WS-1

Spritsail (1) A square sail carried forward, on the bowsprit. It became obsolete in the early XVIII century. Another name for this sail was *blind*, an apt one as the sail obscured visibility ahead. (2) A quadrilateral fore-and-aft sail with its peak supported by a sprit. A fore-and-aft spritsail can be traced back to the second century B.C. (See *Sprit*) A-2, N-1, S-2, WS-1, WAB

Spun Yarn Two or three-stranded small stuff loosely laid, used for various lashings. (e. XVII p.e.) S-2

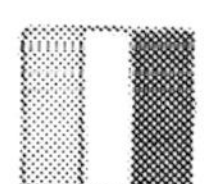

Squall A sudden and often violent wind, sometimes with rain or snow, and of short duration. (e. XVII p.e.) The origin is not certain; it may be from early Swedish or Icelandic, *skvaj*, shout. Squalls can be noisy. DE-3

Squeegee (also *Squilgee,* etc.) A T-shaped device of a board on a long handle, used for getting water off a deck. (XVIII) The origin is not clear but it is probably related to *Soojee*. (XVIII) DE-3

Stack Another name for a funnel on an engine-powered ship. (XIX) The word probably originated in this sense as navy slang. DE-4

Stadimeter An instrument used to measure the horizontal distance to another vessel or to a point ashore. (XIX) It is a composite word, from the Greek *stadion*, a measure of length. DE-5

Stanchion Any of a number of vertical supports for rails, lifelines, or structurally between decks. (XV) An earlier spelling was stantion, which was seen in Anglo-Saxon. Another source was the Old French *estachon*, and this probably came from Late Latin *stantier*, that which stands firm. S-2, WO-1

Stand (1) To steer a course in a given direction. (XVII) (2) To stand a watch is to serve a regular short period of duty. (XVI) The origin in these meanings is uncertain. Source words appear in all the old Teutonic languages, Old English being *standen*. DE-3

Standing Rigging All the fixed rigging of any vessel. (e. XVII p.e.) (See *Running rigging*) S-2

Starboard The right side of any craft when facing the bow. (XIII) Prior to the advent of the stern rudder, vessels had their steering oars on the right, or starboard side. The term appeared recognizably in all the old northern languages and does so in the modern ones. The Anglo-Saxon was *steorbord*, and the Middle English, *sterbord*. S-1, WO-1

Start Said of a line or tackle, to ease it out or to slack it. (XVI) The word came from the Middle English, *sterte*, thence from Old English, *styrten*, both meaning to start, probably in this sense. WO-1

Stateroom An officer's or passenger's cabin on a merchant ship, or the cabin of an officer other than the captain on a naval vessel. One possibility for the origin of this term is that ships of the XVI and XVII centuries often had cabins reserved for important personages, as for royalty and nobility, and such cabins may have been so designated. DE-3

Stay The general term for any of a number of supporting lines, of rope, wire, or bar, to support a mast. The origin could be any or all of Old Norse or Anglo-Saxon *stag*, support, or Old French, *estaye*, prop or support. A-2, WS-1

Staysail A sail, usually triangular, set on a centerline stay. (XVII) The derivation is the same as for stay. A-2

Steer The term needs no definition. (XIII) The word came from early Middle English, *staren*, and goes back to Old Norse and to Anglo-Saxon, the latter, *steoran*, to steer. As is the case for starboard, the word is recognizable in all the Nordic languages. S-1, DE-3

Steerage (1) Earlier the junior officers' quarters in a warship. It was so called because the tiller usually projected into this compartment, which was aft. (XVII) (2) The cheapest and simplest passenger quarters on a liner. (l. XIX) In some ships this compartment was near the stern. (3) The act of steering, also the effect of the helm on a ship. (e. XVII p.e.) (See *Steer*) S-1, S-2, DE-5

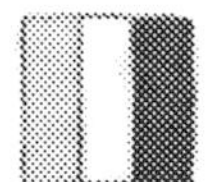

Steeve (See *Stive*) A-2

Stem The upright structural member forming the shape of the bow. (XIV) The Middle English word was *stemn*, the Anglo-Saxon, *stefn*, both of this meaning; a similar word appeared in all the Nordic languages. S-1, WO-1

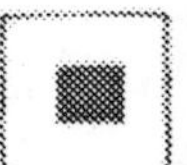

Stemwinder A nickname for the typical Great Lakes cargo steamer, on which the bridge, hence all control, was in the extreme bow—the stem. (e. XX) H-2

Step The base of a mast; also the verb to place a mast in position. (XVII p.e.) The term came from Old English, *staepen*, mast base. M-2, WO-1

Stern The after end of any craft. (XIV) Its origin is the Old Norse *stjorn*, meaning steering. The connection seems apparent. S-1, WO-1

Sternfast A line from the stern to the shore—a sternline; also a stern anchor. (e. XVII p.e.) S-2

Sternpost The structural member in the stern to which the strakes are fastened. (XIV) S-1

Stern Sheets A platform or seat in the stern of a small boat. (XIII) The term sheet in this sense comes from the Old English *skeat*, a floorboard or platform in a boat. S-1, WO-1

Sternson A structural member inboard and in support of the sternpost. (XIV) (See *Keelson, Sternpost*) S-1

Stevedore The man in charge ashore of loading and discharging cargo. (XVIII p.e.) The derivation of this term is early Spanish, *estivador*, earlier the stower of wool and later of any cargo. WO-1

Steward A general term for any member of a ship's crew who is involved with commissary and personal services to all on board. (e. XVII p.e.) An old chief steward may smile over this one; it is derived from the Anglo-Saxon *styweard*, a keeper of the pigs. M-2, WS-1

Stinkpot Now the "rag-sailor's" jocular term for a motorboat, in this modern sense it very likely referred in the late XIX century to early steam launches and their belchings of smoke. The term appeared no later than the mid-XVIII, with a different meaning, it was then a smoke bomb, used in sea combat. Quoting Falconer, "The fuses . . . being lighted, they immediately were thrown upon the deck of the enemy . . . producing an intolerable stench and smoke, filling the said deck with tumult and confusion. . . ." F-1a, K-1, JR

Stirrup A short stout line holding a footrope close to its yard on a square-rigger. (XVII) It may well have got its name because an earlier word for footrope was horse. The word came via Middle English, *stirop*, from Old English, *stigrap*, a mounting rope. M-2, WO-1

Stive A shipwright's and designer's term for the angle of the bowsprit to the deck or to the waterline. (e. XVII p.e.) It was sometimes spelled steeve, and appears to have come from Old English, *stifig*, steep—which the angle often was. A-2, C-8

Stoak To choke, as of the limber holes, pump intakes, and scuppers. (XVII) The derivation is obscure; it could be a corruption of stoke. M-2, WO-1

Stock (1) The crossbar of a stock anchor, hence its name. (IX) M-2, WS-1 (2) The rudder stock is the part of the rudder post that passes through the rudder port or tube, to which the tiller or steering machinery is attached. (XIII) The word comes from the Anglo-Saxon *stoc*, trunk or staff, but probably not with this latter meaning, as stern rudders were then yet to be seen. M-2, WS-1

Stockholm Tar A dark-colored pine tar used yesteryear to coat a ship's topsides, decks, spars, and cordage. (p. XVII) The best of such tars came from Sweden and Norway, and exited the Baltic via Stockholm. D-3

Stocks The blocks and shores upon which a ship or boat is built. (XIII) The origin is Old Norse, *stokken*, of this meaning. B-8, WO-1

Stop (1) A line or strop used in furling a sail, and to keep it furled. (XIX p.e.) It comes from Old English, *stoppa*, a short piece of line. (See *Gasket*) DE-3 (2) A length of light twine or yarn to keep a sail or a flag from flying free until hoisted into proper position. (See *Snotter*)

Stopper A line or chain securely fastened at one end, used to keep another in place, as an anchor stopper. (e. XVII p.e.) M-2, DE-5

Stove In sailors' language, this is the present as well as the past-tense word for smash or smashed. (XIX p.e.) DE-3

Stow To put anything away in its proper place. (e. XVII p.e.) The term was seen in Middle English, *stowen*, of this meaning, and appears to come from early Dutch, *stouwen*, pack, cram. S-2, WS-1

Strake A course of planking or plates that is part of the sides and bottom of a hull. (XV) This term comes from the Old English *streccan*, to stretch. S-1, WO-1

Stream To stream an object, such as a sea anchor or a taffrail log, is simply to run it overboard. (e. XVII p.e.) The word comes intact from Middle and Old English, possibly of this same meaning. M-2, DE-4

"In the stream" is a common term for being moored off the shore—whether or not in a river. (XIX p.e.) B-6

Stream Anchor A light anchor, usually about half the weight of the bowers, used for temporary mooring, warping, and for use astern, (XVII p.e.) Its modern equivalent in the pleasure-boat world is the "lunch hook." S-2, DE-3

Strike To take down or put below. (e. XVII p.e.) The term in this sense comes from the Middle English *strican*, and could have come from Old English.

One never strikes the colors, as this means surrender. (XVI) M-2, WO-1

Strop The sailor's word for a strap. (XIV) The word comes as is from Old English, then meaning a band or thong, and possibly is related to the Greek word *strophus*, twisted cord. It is recognizable in several Nordic languages. WO-1, WS-1

Strum Box A filter for a bilge pump, an old term. (XVII p.e.) It is possibly a corruption of thrum. (See *Rose Box, Thrum*) S-2, WO-1

Studding Sail (Contracted to *Stun's'l*) a sail on a special spar, extending outboard of a square sail or sails, for added sail area in moderate winds. (XVI) An earlier spelling was *stayten sale*. Its origin is not clear; it possibly is from Middle Dutch, *stodinge*, thrust—and that they did add. WO-1

Sundowner A general term for a strict captain or mate who was stingey about granting shore leave. (XIX p.e.) Said of the clipper ships and possibly earlier traders, as well as of naval vessels. K-1, N-4

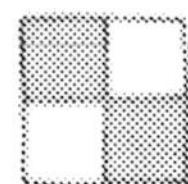

Sun Over the Yardarm When in the olden days of our "wet" Navy it was late enough in the morning for a midday drink. (p.m. XIX) The term is in current use in many pleasure craft and passenger vessels. K-1, N-4, JR

Supercargo An officer or a supernumerary in a merchant ship who was in charge of trading—a seagoing merchant. (XVII) An earlier spelling was supracargo. The term came from the Spanish *sobrecargo*, in charge of cargo. These gentlemen were very important to the success of merchant ships before the advent of rapid communications. WO-1

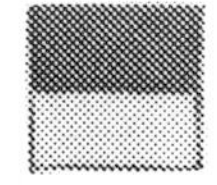

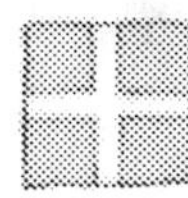

Swab (1) A seagoing mop, also the act of using one. (2) a shipboard drudge or dullard. (Both XVI) The origin of the word is uncertain, but it could be the Dutch *swabber*, a drudge. WO-1

Swallow the Anchor, To Said of a merchant seaman when he quits the sea. The phrase is believed to have originated among British liner officers. (l. XIX) WM-3

Sway A method of applying one's weight to a halyard or other line to get "that extra two inches." (XVIII) The word comes from Middle English, *sweghe*, to sway, possibly in this sense. WS-1

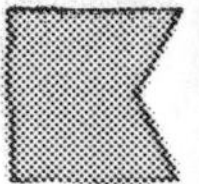

Sweep (1) An oar of a racing shell. (XIX) (2) Any extra-large oar. (XVII p.e.) The term comes from Middle English, *swepe*, long oar. (See *Scull*) WO-1

Swifters Earlier (c. XVI) tackles, or pendants and tackles, augmenting the shrouds of a sailing ship. Later (XVIII) they were the forwardmost shrouds—a natural evolution. (2) Lines rigged to the ends of bars on a capstan to keep them in place, and for extra hands. (XVII) The word came from Old Norse, *svipta*, to reef, also to haul taut. S-1, DE-3

Tabernacle A hinged socket at deck level for a mast, to enable it to be lowered. (XIX p.e.) When the term became a nautical one is uncertain, but masts could be so lowered when changing from sail to oars in the Viking longships. The term probably started as a nickname, because of its appearance. DE-3, JR

Tabling Reinforcement of sail edges and corners, also of covers, awnings, etc. (e. XVII p.e.) The origin is uncertain; the word comes from Middle English, *tablen*, possibly of this sense. S-2, DE-3

Tack (1) The windward clew of a squaresail, also the windward corner of a spinnaker and the forwardmost corner on a fore-and-aft sail. (XV) (2) A "leg" of a course when sailing to windward. (XV) (3) The verb to tack is to turn a sailing craft "through the wind," to take the wind on her other side. (XVI p.e.) The origin of the word is Old French, *tache*, probably of all these meanings. S-2, WO-1

Tackle is a broad term, referring to gear on deck and aloft in general, but more particularly to devices of blocks and their lines and hardware. (p. XIII) The sailor's pronunciation is often "tayckle." The term comes from the Middle Dutch *taekel*, of the latter meaning, and which may account for the traditional pronunication. S-2, W-2, WO-1

Tackline A divider of light line between flags on a signal hoist. (XVIII) Its origin could be from its similarity to a jib or staysail pendant, both called a tack pendant. F-1, N-4

Tackling Perhaps a better word than tackle for the latter's broad meaning, it is a term for all a ship's running rigging. (e. XVII p.e.) It has the same basic origin as tackle. S-2, DE-4

Taffrail The rail around the uppermost deck in the stern of a vessel, earlier as the poop or quarterdeck. (XVII) An earlier spelling was tafferal, which referred more to the then customary ornamental treatment of the stern than to a rail. The term appears to come from the early Dutch *tafereel*, a panel or tablet. Some seamen-types pronounce it "taffr'l." WO-1, WS-1

Tagline A line for steadying a load or a boat on a hoist. (XVII) The term appears to come from the Middle English *taegel*, tail, or the same word in Dutch. DE-3

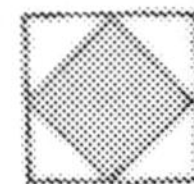

Tail (1) The hauling end of a line, as for a winch or tackle. (XVII p.e.) (2) To tail, or tail on, as to haul in on a line as above, or wherever some extra hands are needed. (XVII) (3) A vessel's action when anchored, such as tailing to the tide or to the wind. (XVII) In all these senses the term could be from Middle English and Dutch, as for *Tagline*. DE-3

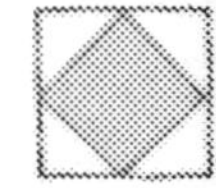

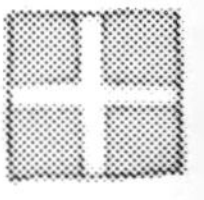

Take Charge Said when a line, spar, sail, or the helm gets out of control, or gets the upper hand. (p. XVI) WP-1c, DE-3

Take the Bottom To run aground. (XVII p.e.) B-4

Tar An old word for a common sailor. (XVIII p.e.) It is believed to come from the fact that these men wore hats and garments of tarred cloth. (See *Stockholm Tar*) WS-1

Tarpaulin Now any heavy canvas or similar synthetic material used for hatch and boat covers, awnings, etc., earlier it was canvas treated with pine tar. (XVII p.e.) Paulin, or pauling, comes from Anglo-Saxon, *paeil*, cover. S-2, WS-1

Taut Tight or snug. (e. XVII p.e.) The term comes from the Middle English word *togt*, pulled tight, and goes back to Old English, *teon*, to pull, and to Anglo-Saxon, *togian*, to draw or pull. S-2, WO-1

Taut Ship is an expression for a ship and her people where everything is done right—or else! (XVIII p.e.) N-4, WO-1

Telltale (1) A compass other than the master or steering compass. (XIX p.e.) (2) A pennant aloft or a streamer in the rigging, to aid the watch officer and the helmsman to detect the behavior of the wind in sailing craft. (XVIII p.e.) (See *Dog Vane*) S-3, DE-3

Tender (1) A small or midsize craft servicing one or more larger vessels, for personnel, supplies, etc., and as a dispatch boat. (XVII p.e.) In this sense the term comes from French and Old French, *tendre*, to aid. WO-1, DE-3 (2) An adjective, describing any craft with low stability. (XVIII p.e.) In this meaning the word also comes from the French *tendre*, meaning tender or delicate. DE-3

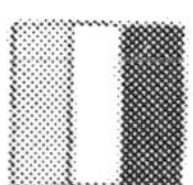

Tern Schooner A three-masted schooner built in New England or Nova Scotia (m.-to-l. XIX) Tern in this sense is a set of three, and comes via Middle English and early French from the Latin *terni*, of this same meaning. M-1, WAB

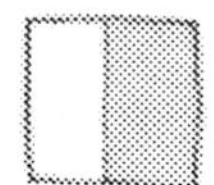

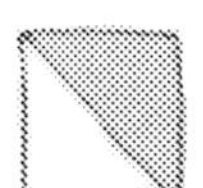

Thimble A heart-shaped or round ring grooved to fit within the eye of spliced rope. (XVII) The word came from Middle English, *thybol*, of this meaning. B-1, DE-5

Thole Pins Pegs set in the gunwales of an oar-propelled boat that serve as a fulcrum for an oar. (XII) Thole comes from Old English, *thol*, oar pin. S-1, WO-1

Thoroughfoot (also ***Throughput***) (1) An old term for a dipped tackle or a tumbled block. (e. XVII p.e.) (2) Coiling a line the wrong way to remove kinks or to bring back its lay. (XVII p.e.) The origin in both of these meanings is not known. S-3

Three Sheets to the Wind is said of sailors, and others, who have over-imbibed. (XVIII) It probably is a corruption of free sheets, implying carelessness. WM-3b

Throat The forwardmost upper corner of a gaff sail, and the forward end of its gaff. (XVIII) The word came from Anglo-Saxon, *protu*, throat in the sense of anything narrow. (See *Nock*) F-1, DE-3

Thrum Short pieces of rope yarn used in making mats; also the act of doing so. The word comes from Old English, one meaning of which was remnant. (XIV) (See *Strum Box*) DE-3, WO-1

Thrum Mat A mat made of canvas with rope-ends or rope yarn worked into it, for chafing gear and patching. (XIV) WS-1

Thurrock An old term for a deep hold, also for the bilge. (XII) It is from Old English, *thurruc*, the bottom of a ship. WO-1

Thwart A seat or crossbeam in a small boat. (XIV) Earlier spellings were thought and thowt. The term comes from the Middle English *thwarte*, across, and possibly originated in Old English. S-1, WO-1

Tide hardly needs definition. (XIV) The word goes back to Old Saxon, *tid*, tide. WO-1

Tide Over This was originally a mariner's term, for alternately sailing and anchoring depending on the tides, to work a ship into or out of a port. (XVIII p.e.) F-1

Tierce A type of cask, also an old measure for wines and provisions. (XVI) It was of forty-two gallons, or one-third of a pipe. The word came from Old French, the same word, meaning one-third, and goes back to Latin. WO-1

Ties An old word for Gaskets or sail stops. (XVII) (See *Gaskets, Stop, Tyes*) S-2, WS-1

Tiller A bar which serves as a lever to turn the rudder. (XV p.e.) Earlier sometime spelled tillar, the word comes via Middle English from *telian*, Anglo-Norse for the arm or lever on a steering oar. S-2, WO-1

Timoneer An old term for helmsman. (e. XVII p.e.) The term comes from the French *timonier*, of this meaning, thence from Late Latin, *timon*, helm. S-2, WO-1

Timonoguy A jackstay to prevent running rigging from fouling with deck gear. (XVII p.e.) The origin is obscure; it probably is from Old French. WO-1

Tingle A metal patch. (p. XIII) The derivation is not known, it appears to be related to the Middle High German word *zingel*, that which fastens. B-1, DE-3

Toggle A short bar spliced into the end of a line, usually to fasten it to another. (e. XVII p.e.) An earlier spelling was tuggle. Its origin is not known. B-8, WW-1

Tom (also *Tomm*) Usually expressed to "tom down," to shore or chock cargo, especially from above. (p. XVIII) The derivation is obscure; it possibly is a corruption of tamp, which comes from the Old French *estamper*, to ram or to tamp. F-1b

Ton (also *Tonnage*) A complete discussion of tons and tonnage is inappropriate for these pages. In general, tonnage is a measure of space rather than weight, this measurement governed by various rules. The only definition for which weight applies is displacement tonnage, the weight of the water displaced by a ship; this measurement being used virtually exclusively for naval ships. Ton is a variation of tun, a wine cask, and the measurement of the cargo capacity of a ship was the number of these she could carry. (XIV) (See *Tun*) K-1, WO-1, WS-1

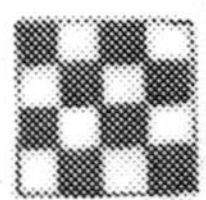

Toothpick A catwalk from the pilothouse or bridge to the forecastle of some small Pacific Coast steamers. (l. XIX or e. XX) It probably got its name because it usually was narrow and tapered. KK

Top A broad term for anything high or above. It is often used as an adjective or prefix.

Topgallant Mast Of a three-part mast, the uppermost section. (XVI) S-1

Topgallant Sails The sails above the topsails of a square-rigger. (p. XV) S-1

Top Hamper Earlier all the spars and rigging, now a ship's superstructure and upper-deck equipment. (XVII) S-2

Top Mark A marker or shape on the top of a buoy or a beacon. (XIV) S-1

Topmast The upper section of a two-part mast, or the middle one of a three-part mast. (XVI) S-1

Top Maul A special mallet or maul for driving a fid into or out of the topmast doubling in a sailing ship. (XVIII) It was so called because it was always kept at the top. WO-1

Topping Lift A line or tackle for lifting the free end of a boom. (XVIII p.e.) F-1

Toprope (also two words or hyphenated) A line or tackle for sending up a topmast. (XVII p.e.) S-2

Tops, The Platforms at the heads of the lower masts of a sailing ship. (XIII) L-1

Topsail On a square-rigger, the second sail, or the second and third sails aloft. (XV) On a fore-and-after, a sail set above the gaff. S-1

Topside The side of a vessel above the waterline. (XVII p.e.) It is another way of saying "on deck." S-2

Touching An old term for sailing a bit too close to the wind. (XVIII p.e.) This is now called pinching. WM-2

Tow (1) To pull another vessel or boat. (XVII p.e.) The derivation could be either or both of the Anglo-Saxon words *tog*, to pull, or *tohline*, tow. S-2, WO-1 (2) Coarse hemp, from which both cordage and sails were made for many years. (XIV) The origin in this sense is Old Saxon, *tou*, flax fiber. S-1, WS-1

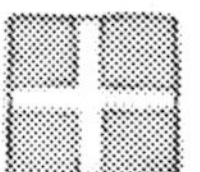

Trade Winds Relatively steady winds, between about 30° latitude and the region of the doldrums near the equator; they are northeast in the northern hemisphere and southeast in the southern. (XVIII) The origin of the term is uncertain; it could well be that in early English any steady wind was so called. DE-5

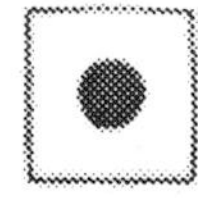

Trailboards Panels at the bows of a sailing vessel, both to brace and to decorate the base of the bowsprit. (XV) An earlier word was *etrayl*, from the Middle English *trayle*, meaning, among other things, to decorate. DE-3

Transfer The distance traveled at right angles to a vessel's original course, on the completion of a 90° turn. The word comes from the Latin *transferre*; when it first had a nautical significance is not known. (See *Advance*) K-2, WS-1

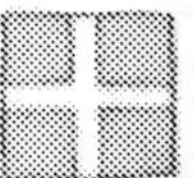

Transom (also *Transome*) (1) The planking or plating across the stern. (XIV) (2) An old term for any 'thwartship beam. (XIV) (3) Sometimes a skylight on deck. (XVII) The Middle English term was *transerseyn*, which came from Old French, *transversin*, cross beam. S-2, WO-1

Traveler Variously defined as a sheet block or as a rail parallel to the deck along which it can slide. (XVII) The word came from Early French, but not in the nautical sense. S-2, DE-5

Trawl (1) A fishing net roughly conical in shape that is dragged near the bottom. (2) To fish with a trawl. (Both XIV p.e.) The term comes from Middle Dutch, *traghel*, a drag net. DE-4

Trawler (1) A type of fishing vessel that uses large bag-like nets, called trawls. (XVI) (2) A sturdy cruising-type motor yacht—in some opinions a misnomer. (m. XX) In this sense the origin of the term may be Old French, *trauler*, to go hither and yon. (See *Trawl*). DE-3, DE-4

Trebling Extra planking in the bows of a wooden vessel, especially for protection agianst ice. (XVIII p.e.) Most ships are double planked. S-3, DE-3

Treenail (also *Trenail, Trunnel*) Pronounced trunnel, a carefully shaped wooden peg by which a wooden craft is sometimes fastened. (XIII) The technique dates from the days of the early Viking ships (VII); the term goes back via Old English to Old Norse, *tre*, tree or wooden, and *nagl*, spike or peg. B-8, S-2

Trestletrees The fore-and-aft timbers at the masthead of a sailing vessel, to support the crosstrees. (XIV) The word trestle came, via Middle English, from Old French, *trestal*, crossbar. A-2, WO-1

Triatic Stay A stay between two masts, earlier for handling cargo and boats as well as to stay the masts themselves. (XVIII p.e.) The name implies a triangle, hence perhaps its origin. S-3, DE-3, JR

Trice (also *Trise, Trize*) To hoist or haul in. (XV) The term came from early Dutch, *trijsen*, of the same meanings. WS-1

Trick One's time on watch or on duty, particularly at the helm (e. XVII p.e.) An earlier word of the same meaning was trike; its origin is early Dutch, *trek*. M-2, DE-3

Trim (1) To haul in, as the sheets or a sail. (XVI) The origin in this sense is probably the Old English word *trymian*, to strengthen. S-2, WO-1 (2) The way a craft lies in the water. In this sense the word came from Anglo-Saxon, *trymman*, to arrange or make firm. S-2, WW-1

Trisail (See *Trysail*)

Truck The top of the uppermost mast, or the extreme masthead. (XVII) An earlier word was truckle, which probably came from the Anglo-French *trockle*, and it from the Greek, *troxos*, both meaning a hoop or ring—to which lines were fastened. A-2, WW-1

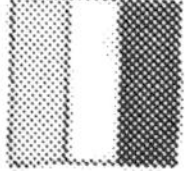

Trunnel (See *Treenail*)

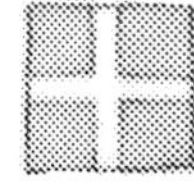

Try An old word, still used, for heaving to. (XV) The origin of the word in this sense is obscure; it could imply trying to keep a ship or boat on a desired heading in adverse conditions. (See *A-Try*) S-2, WO-1

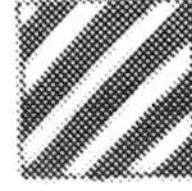

Trysail A triangular fore-and-aft sail used as a steadying sail and in stormy conditions. It was not so named for its shape, as is commonly believed, but because it is used for heaving to. (XVIII p.e.) (See *Try*) WO-1

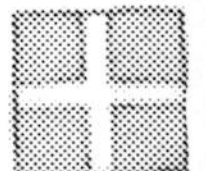

Tuck The shape of the hull aft, where the planking meets the stern structure. (XIV) The word comes from Middle Dutch, *tucken*, of the same meaning. S-2, WO-1

Tug A vessel used in towing. (XIX) These vessels came into being with the steam age, but the word is an old one; it comes from Middle English, *toggen*, to pull. WO-1

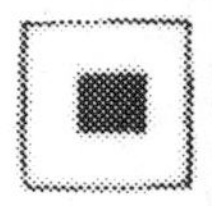

Tumblehome The sloping or curving of a vessel's sides, inboard from the vertical. (e. XVII p.e.) Earlier called falling home and tumbling home. The derivation is not known; it could be from Old French, *tumeresse*. One meaning of tumble in Middle English was to tilt or slope. (See *Home*) F-1, DE-3

Tun A large wine cask, of about 33 cubic feet, which became a standard of measurement for the cargo capacity of a merchant vessel. (XIII) The term goes back to Anglo-Saxon, *tunne*, barrel. (See *Ton*) WO-1

Turn To To go to work. (XVIII p.e.) Turn in this sense meant to direct attention or activity, as to a task. N-4, DE-3

'Tweendecks A partial deck between two full ones, usually just below the main deck. (XVII) The word is simply a corruption of between decks.

Twiddler A line or tackle to the helm, to aid in steering. (XVII) Its origin appears to be from the same word in early English, then slang for help. WO-1

Two-Block (XIX p.e.) (See *Chock-a-Block*)

Tyes Lines connecting the yards of a square-rigger to the tackles by which they were hoisted and lowered. (e. XVII p.e.) The origin is not certain; it may have been Old Norse, *tang*, rope. The Middle English word was *tie*. (See *Ties*) A-2, DE-4

Typhoon A strong tropical storm in the Pacific area. (XVIII) The origin of the word is uncertain; a good probability is *ta fung*, Cantonese for gale. WS-1

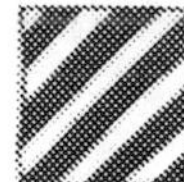

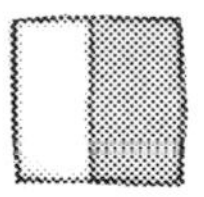

U-Boat A German submarine. (e. XX) It comes from the German *Unterseeboot*, literally under-sea boat. DE-5

Vang (1) A line to steady or control the gaff of a fore-and-aft sail. (XVII p.e.) The origin is probably Dutch. M-2, WO-1 (2) A line or tackle to hold the boom down in a racing sailboat. (XIX) The word came from the same one in Dutch, of the first meaning.

'Vast A salty aphetic of *Avast*.

Veer (1) To run out a line. (XV) In this sense the word comes from Middle English, *vieren*, to let out or slack. (2) To change course. (XVI) Here the origin, via Old French, *virer*, is the Latin *vertere*, turn. (3) Of the wind, to change in direction counterclockwise. (e. XVII p.e.) It probably came from Old French in this sense, also *virer*. M-2, WO-1

Verdigris The greenish patina on copper and copper alloys from salt water. (e. XIV) The term comes from the Old French *vert de Grece*, the green of Greece. (Why Greece, particularly, is anyone's guess.) WO-1

Very Pistol A pistol from which cartridges containing colored flares can be fired. (XIX) It was named for its inventor, Samuel W. Very, a naval officer. DE-4

Vessel A general term for any large craft. (XIII) The word comes from Old French, *vaissel*, also *vaisseau*, for ship or large craft. It goes back further, to Latin, but whether in a nautical sense is not certain. WO-1, DE-3

Voyage A course of travel by water. (XIII) Its derivation is Latin, *viaticum*, travel money; it came into English from Old French, *voyage*, of the modern meaning. WO-1

Voyal (also *Viol*) An old term for the messenger nipped to the anchor cable; it was the line that actually was worked by the capstan. (e. XVII p.e.) This was also the name for a large block used in this function. The origin of the term is not known. (See *Nipper*) DE-3

Waist The center, or 'midship section of a ship, twixt bow and stern areas. (XV) The origin of the term is Old English, *veast*, and from it came the Middle English *wast*, both of the same meaning. S-2, WO-1

Wake The track of waves created by a moving craft. (e. XVII p.e.) The term goes back to Old Saxon, *wakon*, and to Old Norse, *waken*, the space made in ice by a ship underway. S-2, WO-1

Wale Any of a number of strakes or additional courses of planking on the topsides of a vessel. (XIII) The word comes from Old English, *walen*, ridge, also from Old Norse, *vala*, knuckle. (See *Channel, Gunwale, Knuckle*) S-1, WO-1

Wardroom The mess and common room for officers in a warship. (p. XVI) Ward comes from the Middle English *warde*, thence Old English *weard*, for warden or watch officer. DE-3

Warp (1) To move a vessel at a pier or dock by the use of lines, also to move a vessel by kedging. (2) The line used in warping. (Both XVII p.e.) The term comes from Old English, *wearpen*, of the same general meaning. M-2, DE-4

Watch A period of time on duty. (XIV) From the Middle English *wacche*, the word goes back to Anglo-Saxon, *waecce*, a watch or guard. S-2, WS-1

Waterborne To be set afloat, or to be afloat. (e. XVII p.e.) Earlier the term was in two words. S-2

Watersail (1) One of several types of spritsails. (XIV) (2) A low studding sail or a sail under the bowsprit of a clipper ship. (XIX) All were aptly named, as they were near the water and had a tendency to get wet. S-1

Waveson An old term for jettisoned cargo and gear left floating. (XVI) Earlier the term was seen as waiveson. The origin is uncertain; it could be Anglo-French, *weive*, give up. S-3, DE-5

Way To be in motion over the bottom. (XVI p.e.) The term under way was seen in the XVII. The term comes from Middle and Old English, *weg*, of this meaning, and is believed to have applied first to ships. WO-1

Ways The shoreside structure in which a ship is built, also called shipways. (XV) The origin is believed to be the Old English *weg*, of this meaning among many others. (See *Cradle, Slipway*) DE-5

Wear To wear ship is to turn a square-rigger before the wind, as in jibing a fore-and-after. (e. XVII p.e.) Older spellings were weare and wager. The term may have come from the French *virer*, to turn. WO-1

Weathercloth Canvas rigged over the bulwarks or rails to protect people and gear from wind and wave. (e. XVIII p.e.) (See *Dodger*) M-3

Weathercock An old term for a vessel that tended to turn into the wind or carried a heavy weather helm. (p. XIII) The Middle English word was *wedercoc*. It may be of interest that the term is now used in relation to aircraft and missiles. B-1, DE-4

Weigh Anchor, To To hoist the anchor. (XIV p.e.) The origin of weigh in this sense is very probably Old Icelandic, *vega*, to lift or carry. (See *Aweigh*) S-1, WO-1

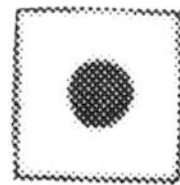

Welin Davit A patented type of quadrantal boat davit that preceded the gravity davit. (e. XX) It got its name from its inventor. K-2

Wending An old term for tacking. (p. XV) The origin of this term is the Anglo-Saxon *wealan*, turn. WS-1, WW-1

Wharf A structure extending from shore to which craft can go alongside. (XV) The term is from late Old English, *hwearf*, of this meaning. (See *Pier*) WW-1

Wheel (1) The first use of a wheel as a helm appears to have been in the late XVII century. (See *Whipstaff*) (2) The nickname for a propeller. (l. XIX) L-1, T-1

Wheft (also *Eaft, Weft,* etc.) A flag or pennant, sometimes tied or stopped in the center of the fly; a signal of various meanings, one of which is believed to have been distress. (XV) The origin is obscure; it is probably Anglo-Saxon. B-6, D-3, DE-3

Whelps Ridges on the drums of capstans, gipsies, etc., to reduce slippage. (e. XVII p.e.) The term is derived from the Middle English *hwelp*, of the same meaning, and may go back to Old English. M-2, DE-3

Wherry (1) Any of a variety of light small rowing boats, usually open. (XV) Earlier wherries often were used as ferries and shore boats. The term comes from the Scottish *whirry*, to hurry. WO-1 (2) In British waters, a small coastal sailing cargo vessel of shoal draft. (p. XVIII)

Whip (1) A simple tackle of one or two single blocks. (e. XVII p.e.) The origin in this sense is obscure. (2) To wrap the end of a line to prevent its fraying or fagging. (p. XIV) The Middle English word was *whippen*, of this same meaning. M-2, DE-4

Whipstaff A vertical steering lever attached to the tiller of a sailing ship, generally in use from the XVI to the early XVIII century. The origin is not known; whip could be from early German, *wippen*, to move, as back and forth. (See *Wheel*) M-2, DE-4

Whiskers (also *Whisker Booms* and *Shrouds*) Lateral bracing to the bowsprit and jibboom of a sailing craft. (e. XIX p.e.) One guess is that it was a nickname, from the similarity to dogs' and cats' whiskers. S-3, DE-3, Conjecture

Whitehall Boat A fine-lined rowing boat of many purposes. (e. XIX) These handsome sea-kindly boats were named for Whitehall Street in New York at the foot of which the early ones were based, for ferrying pilots, also chandlers' and agents' representatives, to incoming ships. DE-5, JG

Widowmaker The name given to the long, low-stived bowsprit on a New England fishing schooner. (l. XIX) To be out on one in heavy seas was not a safe place to be. (See *Knockabout*) C-4

Wildcat The drum on a windlass with grooves and projections to engage anchor chain. (XIX) The origin of the term is not known, but it is wise not to get too close when the anchor is "let go." DE-5

Williamson Turn A formalized maneuver to turn a craft to put her on an exact reverse course, especially to recover a man overboard. (m. XX) It was named for John A. Williamson, then a reserve officer in the "subchaser navy," who developed it (ca. 1943). Pub-5

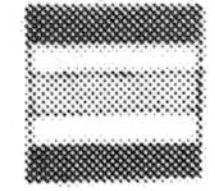

Winch An "engine" for hoisting and hauling. (XVI p.e.) The origin of this term is the Anglo-Saxon *wince*, a crank or handle. WO-1

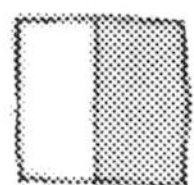

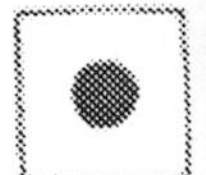

Wind The word comes to us intact from Old English and Old Saxon. (XI p.e.) The Old Norse word was *windr*, wind or winds. WO-1

Windfall The original meaning was simply a tree felled by the wind. The nautical significance was that standing trees of a certain size, regardless of where located, in Great Britain and the then-colonies, belonged to the Crown for shipbuilding. (XVII p.e.) Trees blown down could be claimed and used freely by the landowner. WM-3b

Windjammer A late-XIX century sailing ship, usually a square-rigger. The word is believed to be newsmen's jargon, and was rarely heard from deepwater sailors. DE-5, Pub-1

Windlass A device for hoisting an anchor. (e. XVII p.e.) Earlier it was mounted aft, and used to control what then could be called a backstay. An earlier spelling was windelas. Its origin appears to be Middle English, *windas*, of the same meaning. S-1, DE-3

Windrose (1) The compass rose on a chart, dating before the days of the magnetic needle. (XIV) It pictured the various prevailing winds in an area. (2) A diagram, or a "rose," on a weather chart, indicating directions, velocities, and frequency of winds in a location in a given period of time. (XIX p.e.) K-1, L-3

Windsail A ventilator, consisting of a canvas tube with a cowl or hood, to get fresh air into compartments and holds below. (XVIII p.e.) F-1

Woodlock A hardwood timber, often sheathed, on the rudderpost of a wooden vessel, to prevent the rudder pintles from lifting out. (XVIII p.e.) F-1b

Woold (also *Woolding*) Extra lashing around a spar, especially one that has been fished. (XIV) An earlier spelling was wole. The term comes from the early Dutch *woeling*, of the same meaning. (See ***Fish***) S-1, M-2, WW-1

Workaway A merchant seaman, not a member of a crew, who works with the crew to pay his passage from one port to another. (XIX p.e.) It was originally a merchant-service slang term. H-2, JR

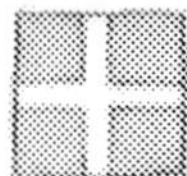

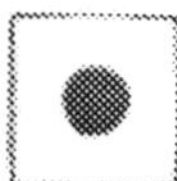

Worming To lay small stuff in the grooves or contlines of rope, preparatory to parcelling and serving. (e. XVII p.e.) It probably is simply a whimsical word from the appearance of the material used. M-2, DE-3

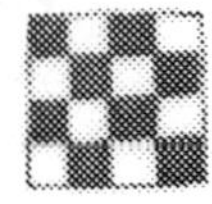

Wrinkle An improvisation or idea to solve a problem. (e. XVIII p.e.) The term in this sense comes from the Anglo-Saxon *wrenc*, meaning a trick or idea. (See *Gilguy*) DE-3

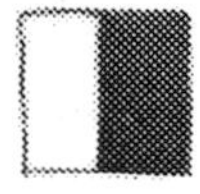

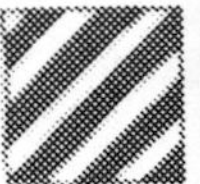

Yacht A privately-owned pleasure boat. (XVII) Earlier a yacht was a vessel of state, for royalty, nobility, and other dignitaries. There are several possible sources for the origin of the word, the most likely of which is the Dutch *jacht*, later *jagt*, from their word *jagten*, speed. WO-1

Yankee Other than the usual American meaning, this was the name of a large jib topsail carried by some American racing yachts, copied and so named by the British. (l. XIX) B-6, JR

Yard A 'thwartship spar for any square sail. (XV p.e.) The term comes from the Anglo-Saxon *seglegerld*, meaning sail yard. S-1, WO-1

Yardarm (1) The outer portion or the tip of a yard. (XV) S-1, DE-3 (2) Now too, a'thwartship spar on the mast of a naval or merchant ship or a smaller power-boat, for signals, etc. JR

Yare An old and rare term for shipshape and nimble. (p. IX) The origin is Old English, *gearu*, of this meaning. W-2, DE-3

Yarn (1) Strands of thread twisted together, loosely for some purposes, hard and tight for others, as for making rope. (XVI p.e.) The origin of the term in this sense is the Anglo-Saxon *gearn*, of the same meaning. (2) A story or chat. (XVIII p.e.) It is believed to be of nautical origin, but the derivation is not known. DE-3

Yaw To swing off course due to bad steering or difficult sea conditions. (e. XVIII p.e.) One possible source is Icelandic, *jaga*, to go to and fro; another, Old Norse, is *ga*, to bend from the course. S-2, WS-1

Yawl Now a sailboat rig, with a large mainsail forward and a smaller mizzen or jigger aft. (m. or l. XIX) (2) A utility boat, sometimes called a yawlboat. (XVIII p.e.) The derivation of the word is uncertain; it could be from the Dutch *jol,* Middle German *jolle*, or French *yale*, possibly all three, and all in the latter sense. WO-1

Yeoman An enlisted rating in the Navy and Coast Guard, and a person in a merchant ship, all of whom do clerical work. (e. XIX) The word goes back to early Middle English, but its origin in the nautical sense is obscure. K-1, N-4

Zenith The highest point in the sky in its transit, of a celestial body. The term comes, via Middle English *senyth*, from Old French, *cenith*, and from Old Saxon, *szenith*, all of the same meaning. It could go back to Arabic, *samturas*, high point in the heavens. WS-1

Appendix I: Older Spellings of Currently Used Terms

The following are only samplings, in both columns, in the ''old'' especially. There are many variations; a few of the old terms were quite different.

Modern	*Old*
bilge	billage
binnacle	bittacle
bulkhead	bulke head
cabin	cabbin(e)
capstan	captaine
channels	chaine wailes
clew	clue
coil	quoile
deck	decke
dunnage	dinnage
fathom	fadome
fluke	flook
floor	rung
futtock	foot hook
gunwale	gun waile
hoist	hoise
launch(n)	launce
loggerhead	loggerheat
parcelling	parsling
reeve	rive
ringbolt	wrain bolt
seize	seaze
serve	sarve
sheave	shiver
skeg	skek
taffrail	tafferel
taut	taught
wale	waile
windlass	windas

There are many more — some rather farfetched and some obvious. The old spellings are in some cases keys to modern pronunciations.

Appendix II: Corrections of Sea Terms

Corruptions of words in the development of sailors' language have been a way of life and have survived for many centuries. It is hoped that some of the recent ones heard and seen in the pleasure-boat world will not survive, as being less than desirable. Here are a few.

AFT as an adjective, as in aft cabin. The correct adjective is after; aft is an adverb.

BUMPER is often used for fender. See FENDER in the text.

CRAFTS is incorrect for things that float. For these the word is craft, both singular and plural.

HELMING appears to be a newsman's word for steering. There is such a word, but one dictionary says it is archaic.

FLYBRIDGE is a short-cut of flying bridge, probably evolving from boat-for-sale advertisements. It is my hope this is the only way the word will be used.

SEDAN for a motorboat with a cabinhouse. I wish the word could be kept ashore, where it belongs.

SALON is a corruption of saloon — not a den of iniquity on shipboard. It too should be kept ashore. See SALOON in the text.

STAIRS, sometimes heard or seen relating to small craft; wrong to the purist. These are for large yachts and passenger ships. (See LADDER in the text.)

TILLERING seems to be another newsman's word for steering, sometimes even referring to racing sailboats that have wheels. There is no such word.

Appendix III: Ropes

Much has been said and written about ropes vs. lines on a ship of yesteryear. Far be it from me to lay the matter to rest (utterly impossible), but here are the names of many of the ropes of sailing-ship days. Those few generally surviving today are indicated with an asterisk. Some are mentioned in the foregoing text.

BACK ROPE A rope, or chain, to stay the dolphin striker.
BELL ROPE* The lanyard on a ship's bell.
BOLT ROPE* The cordage border on virtually every sail, also of an awning.
BUCKET ROPE The line to a bucket, especially if dipped over the side.
BULL ROPE* (a) Used for winging cargo.
(b) A preventer for a mooring buoy.
(c) Another word for a guest warp.
BUOY ROPE* A line to an anchor buoy.
CHECK ROPE A rope stopper.
CHEST ROPE A long line from well forward to a side port or entry ladder.
DAVIT ROPE A line from the cat davit to an anchor's crown or balance-ring.
FOOT ROPE* A "rope," now wire or rod, under a yard, for a seaman's footing aloft.
GUESS ROPE* See guest warp in the text.
HEAD ROPE (a) The bolt rope at the head of a square sail.
(b) A line from the bow of a ship, for warping.
HOOK ROPE* A long light line with a hook spliced into one end.
JACK ROPE A jackstay made of rope.
LEECH ROPE The bolt rope on the leech of a square sail.
LUFF ROPE The bolt rope on the luff of a sail.
MANROPE* A safety line for a variety of over-the-side ladders.
MONKEY ROPE A safety line or harness for a man working over the side (standard gear for whalemen).
PARREL ROPE A collar attached to the center of a yard to hold it to its mast, also on the jaws of a gaff.
PASSING ROPE Another term for PASSAREE. (See text)
RING ROPE A rope stopper.
RUDDER ROPES* See yoke ropes, below.
TILLER ROPES The ropes from the wheel drum to the tiller.
TILTING ROPE A guy to an awning.
TOPROPE A line used in sending up or down an upper mast of a sailing ship.
YARD ROPE A line used for hoisting or lowering a yard that is usually fixed in position.
YOKE ROPES* Lines to the rudder yoke on a ship's boat.

Nautical Subjects

A-1 Ansted, Upcott N. *Dictionary of Sea Terms*. Glasgow: 1938.

A-2 Anderson, R.C. *The Rigging of Ships, 1600–1720*. Salem: Marine Research Society, 1927.

A-3a Ashley, Clifford W. *The Ashley Book of Knots*. Garden City, N.Y.: Doubleday & Company, 1944.

A-3b ———. *The Yankee Whaler*. Boston: Houghton Mifflin, 1926.

B-1 Bathe, Basil W., ed. *Visual Encyclopedia of Nautical Terms Under Sail*. New York: Crown Publishers, 1978.

B-2 Beck, Horace. *Folklore and the Sea*. Middletown, Conn: Wesleyan University Press for Mystic Seaport, 1973.

B-3 Biddlecombe, George, ed. *The Art of Rigging*. Salem: Marine Research Society, 1925. (Adapted from David Steel's *Elements and Practice of Rigging and Seamanship*, London, 1794.)

B-4 Blanckley, Thomas R. *Naval Expositor*. London: F. Owen, 1750.

B-5 Bowditch, Nathaniel. *American Practical Navigator,* 10th ed. Washington, D.C.: U.S. Hydrographic Office, 1938. (Originally published 1802.)

B-6 Bradford, Gershom. *The Mariner's Dictionary,* 3rd. ed. Barre, Mass.: Barre Publishers, 1972.

B-7 Brewington, Marion V. *Chesapeake Bay Log Canoes and Bugeyes.* Cambridge, Md.: Cornell Maritime Press, 1963.

B-8 Brøgger, Anton W., and Shetelig, Haakon. *The Viking Ships.* Oslo: Dreyers forlag, 1951.

B-9 Burgess, F.H. *A Dictionary of Sailing*. Baltimore: Penguin Books, 1961.

B-10 Bushell, Charles. *The Rigger's Guide and Seaman's Assistant.* Landport, England: E. Annett, 1858.

C-1a Chapelle, Howard I. *The American Fishing Schooners, 1825–1935.* New York: W.W. Norton, 1973.

C-1b ———. *American Small Sailing Craft.* New York: W.W. Norton, 1951.

C-1c ———. *Boat Building.* New York: W.W. Norton, 1941.

C-1d ———. *The History of the American Sailing Navy*. New York: W.W. Norton, 1949.

C-1e ———. *The History of American Sailing Ships*. New York: W.W. Norton, 1935.

C-1f ———. *The Search for Speed Under Sail, 1700–1855.* New York: W.W. Norton, 1967.

C-1g ———. *Yacht Designing and Planning.* New York: W.W. Norton, 1936.

C-2 Colcord, Joanna. ***Sea Language Comes Ashore.*** Cambridge, Md.: Cornell Maritime Press, 1945.

C-3 Craig, Hardin, Jr. ***Bibliography of Encyclopedias and Dictionaries Dealing with Military, Naval and Maritime Affairs, 1577–1965,*** 3rd. ed. Houston: Rice University, 1965.

C-4 Church, Albert Cook. ***The American Fisherman.*** New York: W. W. Norton, 1938.

D-1 Dana, Richard Henry. ***Dana's Seamen's Friend.*** James Lees, ed. London: George Philip & Son, 1856.

D-2 Davis, Charles G. ***The Ship Model Builder's Assistant.*** Salem: Marine Research Society, 1926.

D-3 De Kerchove, Rene. ***International Maritime Dictionary.*** New York: D. Van Nostrand Company, 1961.

F-1a Falconer, William. ***Old Wooden Walls.*** London: W. & G. Foyle, 1930. (Abridged edition of ***An Universal Dictionary of the Marine***, London, 1769.)

F-1b ———. ***Universal Dictionary of the Marine.*** London: 1970. (Reprint of 1780 edition.)

H-1 Hahn, Harold M. ***The Colonial Schooners, 1763–1775.*** Annapolis: U.S. Naval Institute Press, 1981.

H-2 Hall, Ernie. ***Flotsam, Jetsam and Lagan from the Seven Seas, the Five Great Lakes and Our Inland Rivers.*** Cambridge, Md.: Cornell Maritime Press, 1965.

H-3 Harbord, Rev. John B. ***Glossary of Navigation.*** Portsmouth, England, 1883.

H-4 Heinl, Robert D., Jr. ***Dictionary of Military and Naval Quotations.*** Annapolis: U.S. Naval Institute Press, 1978.

H-5 Henderson, Richard. ***The Cruiser's Compendium.*** Chicago: Regnery, 1973.

J-1 Jobé, Joseph, ed. ***The Great Age of Sail.*** Lausanne: Edita, 1967.

K-1 Kemp, Peter, ed. ***Oxford Companion to Ships and the Sea.*** London: Oxford University Press, 1976.

K-2 Knight, A.M. ***Modern Seamanship,*** 10th ed. New York: D. Van Nostrand, 1941.

L-1 Landström, Björn. ***The Ship.*** New York: Doubleday, 1961.

L-2 Lane, Carl D. ***The Boatman's Manual,*** 4th ed. New York: W.W. Norton, 1979.

L-3 Layton, Cyril W.T. ***Dictionary of Nautical Words and Terms.*** Glasgow: Brown, Son & Ferguson, 1955.

L-4 Leslie, Robert C. ***Old Sea Wings, Ways, and Words.*** London: Chapman & Hall, 1890.

L-5 Lever, Darcy. *Young Officer's Sheet Anchor.* Providence: Ship Model Society of Rhode Island, 1930. (Originally published London 1808.)

L-6 Longridge, Charles Nepean. *The Anatomy of Nelson's Ships.* London: P. Marshall, 1955.

L-7 Lott, Arnold S. *Almanac of Naval Facts.* Annapolis: U.S. Naval Institute Press, 1964.

L-8 Lovette, Leland P. *Naval Customs, Traditions and Usage.* Annapolis: U.S. Naval Institute Press, 1934.

M-1 MacEwen, William A., and Lewis, Alice H. *Encyclopedia of Nautical Knowledge.* Cambridge, Md.: Cornell Maritime Press, 1953.

M-2 Manwayring, George E., ed. *The Life and Works of Sir Henry Manwayring*, vols. I, II. London, 1920. Note: Manwayring is also spelled Mainwaring. His work was originally done 1620–23 and published in 1644.

M-3 Moore, J.J. *Mariner's Dictionary*. Washington, D.C.: William Duane, 1805.

M-4 Morris, Edward P. *The Fore-and-Aft Rig in America.* New Haven: Yale University Press, 1927.

M-5 Martin, Tyrone G. *A Most Fortunate Ship*. Chester, Conn.: Globe Pequot Press, 1980.

N-1 Noel, John V. *Boating Dictionary.* New York: Van Nostrand Reinhold, 1981.

N-2 ———. *Dictionary of Ships and the Sea.* New York: Van Nostrand Reinhold, 1981.

N-3 Noel, John V., and Bassett, Frank E. *Knight's Modern Seamanship*, 16th ed. New York: Van Nostrand Reinhold, 1977.

N-4 Noel, John V., and Beach, E. L. *Naval Terms Dictionary,* 4th ed. Annapolis: U.S. Naval Institute Press, 1978.

N-5 Norie, John W. *Naval Dictionary.* London, 1804.

P-1a Paasch, Heinrich. *From Keel to Truck.* Antwerp: Ratinckx Frères, 1885.

P-1b ———. *Illustrated Marine Encyclopedia.* London, 1910.

P-2 Patterson, Howard. *Patterson's Illustrated Nautical Encyclopedia.* Cleveland: Marine Review Publishing Co., 1901.

R-1 Rigg, H.K. *Rigg's Handbook of Nautical Etiquette.* New York: Alfred A. Knopf, 1970.

R-2 Rosenfeld, Stanley Z., and Taylor, William H. *The Story of American Yachting.* New York: Appleton-Century-Crofts, 1958.

R-3 Rousmaniere, John. *Glossary of Modern Sailing Terms.* New York: Dodd, Mead, 1976.

R-4 Russell, W. Clark. *Sailor's Language.* London: Sampson Low, 1883.

S-1 Sandahl, K.O. Bertil. *Middle English Sea Terms.* Upsala, Sweden: Lundequistska Bokhandelin; Cambridge, Mass.: Harvard University Press, 1951.
S-2 Smith, John. *A Sea-mans Grammar and Dictionary.* London, 1627.
S-3 Smyth, William H. *The Sailor's Word-Book.* London: Blackie & Son, 1867.
T-1 Tre Trykare. *The Lore of Ships.* New York: Holt, Rinehart & Winston, 1963.
T-2 Turpin, Edward A., and MacEwen, William A. *Merchant Marine Officers' Handbook.* New York: Cornell Maritime Press, 1945.
U-1a Underhill, Harold A. *Sailing Ship Rigs and Rigging.* Glasgow: Brown, Son & Ferguson, 1938.
U-1b ———. *Masting and Rigging the Clipper Ship & Ocean Carrier.* Glasgow: Brown, Son & Ferguson, 1946.
V-1a Villiers, Alan J. *Men, Ships, and the Sea.* Washington, D.C.: National Geographic Society, 1962.
V-1b ———. *The Way of a Ship.* New York: Scribner's, 1953.
W-1 Watson, G.O. *Marine Engineering and Nautical Terms.* London: Geo. Newmes, Ltd., 1964.
W-2 Whall, W.B. *Shakespeare's Sea Terms Explained.* Bristol, England: J.W. Arrowsmith, 1910.
Y-1 Young, Arthur. *Nautical Dictionary.* London, 1863.

On Words

WF-1 Funk, Wilfred. *Word Origins.* New York: Funk & Wagnall, 1963.
WK-1 Klein, Ernest. *A Comprehensive Etymological Dictionary of the English Language.* Amsterdam: Elsevier, 1966.
WM-1 Mencken, H.L. *The American Language,* 4th ed. New York: Alfred A. Knopf, 1936.
WM-2 Moore. *You English Words.* Philadelphia: Lippincott, 1961.
WM-3a Morris, William and Mary. *Dictionary of Word and Phrase Origins,* vols. 1, 2. New York: Harper & Row, 1962, 1967.
WM-3b ———. *Morris Dictionary of Word and Phrase Origins.* New York: Harper & Row, 1977.
WO-1 Onions, Charles T., ed. *Oxford Dictionary of English Etymology.* Oxford: Clarendon Press, 1966.
WP-1a Partridge, Eric. *A Dictionary of Slang and Unconventional English,* 7th ed. New York: Macmillan Co., 1970.

WP-1b ———. *The Gentle Art of Lexicography.* New York: 1963.

WP-1c ———. *Origins,* 4th ed. New York: Macmillan Co., 1977.

WP-2a Pei, Mario. *The Many Hues of English.* New York: Alfred A. Knopf, 1967.

WP-2b ———. *The Story of Language*, rev. ed. Philadelphia: Lippincott, 1965.

WR-1 Radford, Edwin. *Unusual Words.* New York: Philosophical Library, 1946.

WS-1 Skeat, Walter William. *An Etymological Dictionary of the English Language*, 4th ed. Oxford: Clarendon Press, 1910.

WS-2 Smith, Logan P. *Words and Idioms.* London: Constable & Co., 1925.

WW-1 Weekley, Ernest. *An Etymological Dictionary of Modern English*, vols. 1, 2. New York: Dutton, 1921; reprint, New York: Dover, 1967.

Dictionaries and Encyclopedias

DE-1 *Encyclopaedia Britannica*, 1946 edition.

DE-2 *New Columbia Encyclopedia*, 1975 edition.

DE-3 *New English Dictionary (Oxford English Dictionary), 1933.*

DE-4 *Random House Dictionary*, 1966.

DE-5 *Webster's Third International Dictionary*, 1961.

Periodicals

Pub-1 *The American Neptune.*

Pub-2 *The Mariner's Mirror.*

Pub-3 *Newport Newstory.*

Pub-4 *U.S. Coast Guard Safety Council Proceedings.*

Pub-5 *U.S. Naval Institute Proceedings.*

Pub-6 *Nautical Research Journal.*

Non-Print Sources

DVR Capt. Donald V. Reardon, USCG (ret.).

JG John Gardner, Mystic Seaport.

JR John Rogers.

KK Karl Kortum, San Francisco.

NMMG National Maritime Museum, Greenwich, England.

RN Royal Navy, various sources.

USCG U.S. Coast Guard, various sources.

USN U.S. Navy, various sources.

WAB William A. Baker, Hingham, Mass.

WWT Warwick W. Tompkins, Jr.

Index to Origins of Sea Terms by Subject Classifications

For the reader who may be interested in one or more categories of terms, following are such (partial) groupings.

Craft Types

Engines

Ground Tackle

Hull

Natural Phenomena

Naval Terms

Navigation and Related Terms

People, Their Life and Functions

Rigs and Rigging

Rigs and Rigging (cont'd)

Ropes and Cordage

Sails and Sailing

Sails and Sailing (cont'd)

Small Craft

Tools and Equipment